MASTER SCHOOL OF MODERN PIANO PLAYING & VIRTUOSITY

MASTER SCHOOL OF MODERN PIANO PLAYING & VIRTUOSITY

ALBERTO JONAS

GYAN

Published by

Gyan Publishing House
5, Ansari Road
Daryaganj, New Delhi-110002
Phone: 011-47034999, 9811692060
E-mail: books@gyanbooks.com

Distribution Network
gyanbooks.com
India, USA, Canada, UK, Australia

ISBN: 978-93-7225-317-7 (HB)

First Published, 1922

2nd Impression 2026

Printed at: Gyan Press, Delhi.

MASTER SCHOOL OF MODERN PIANO PLAYING & VIRTUOSITY
Author: ALBERTO JONAS

The Author & His Collaborators

Master School
of
Modern Piano Playing & Virtuosity
by
Alberto Jonás

A universal method—technical, esthetic and artistic—for the development of pianistic virtuosity.

With original exercises specially written for this work

by

Wilhelm Bachaus—Fannie Bloomfield-Zeisler—Ferruccio Busoni Alfred Cortot—Ernst von Dohnányi—Arthur Friedheim—Ignaz Friedman — Ossip Gabrilowitsch—Rudolph Ganz — Katherine Goodson—Leopold Godowsky—Josef 'Lhevinne—Isidore Philipp — Moriz Rosenthal — Emil von Sauer—Leopold Schmidt— —Sigismond Stojowski.

English, German, French and Spanish Text

by

The Author

In Seven Books

Price Complete $30.00
Single Books I—VI @ $4.50

Book VII (English *or* Spanish) $3.00
Also published in French and German

CARL FISCHER, Inc.
BOSTON NEW YORK CHICAGO

Alberto Jonás

ALBERTO JONÁS

Master School of Modern Piano Playing
AND VIRTUOSITY

Book VII

TABLE OF CONTENTS

TABLE OF CONTENTS

(Continued)

TABLE OF CONTENTS OF ALL THE OTHER BOOKS WILL BE FOUND AT THE END OF THIS VOLUME.

EXERCISES FOR FINGERS WRISTS AND ARMS AWAY FROM THE PIANO

Exercises for Fingers, Wrists and Arms Away from the Piano

IT has always been the hope of every aspiring pianist to discover some gymnastic exercises, away from the piano, that would so strengthen his fingers, hands and arms and render them so supple as not to make it necessary for him to practise technical exercises on the piano. Let it be said at the outset that such a hope can never be fulfilled. Nothing can replace work accomplished at the keyboard.

The flexibility and strength which are required when playing the piano are *sui generis,* that is to say, peculiar to the nature, resources and demands of that instrument; these requirements (strength and flexibility) are different in quality on other musical instruments.

Still, it cannot be gainsaid that there are a few gymnastic exercises which, if indulged in with moderation and intelligence, will make the hand flexible and strong in a way that is helpful for the acquisition of a pianistic technic.

The object of many of these gymnastic exercises accomplished away from the piano consists in increasing the stretch between the fingers and the reach of the hand (from thumb to fifth finger). In order to obtain these results, most pianists pull their fingers apart and press their hand, opened wide, firmly against a table or any other hard surface. It may be asserted, however, that very little good is to be derived from these proceedings and that they are likely to do harm by weakening the ligaments and tendons of the hand.

These ligaments, which bind the fingers to each other, should not be stretched unduly, lest their contracting power becomes affected. Simply "pulling" the fingers apart is apt to bring about this deplorable result. Besides, while endeavoring to stretch the fingers in the manner described, the ligaments remain *passive* and the momentary gain in stretch is followed by a greater contraction of the ligaments and by stiffness and fatigue of the joints.

Quite dangerous and harmful is the practice of inserting pieces of cork or of felt between the fingers. The various stretching machines which have been devised are also dangerous and do more harm than good.

The example of Robert Schumann who crippled his hand permanently in his endeavor to make the fourth finger of his right hand more flexible by violent means will ever remain a warning.

It would seem unnecessary to say that a surgical operation—cutting the skin between the fingers—should not for a moment be given serious thought, were it not that I have found many persons who believe that such an operation would increase the stretch between their fingers. Of all harmful devices it is the very worst.

Stretching Exercises

The following hand gymnastics, done away from the piano, I believe the best for increasing the stretch of the hand and also the stretch between the fingers. They promote flexibility of the ligaments and tendons and benefit the hand in a general way.

Bring the thumb of your left hand in contact with the tip of the 5th finger of the same hand. Place them both, thumb and fifth finger, between the second and third finger of your right hand, half-way between the tip and the root of the fingers. Now turn slightly your right hand. from side to side, in such a way that the hand "gives" at the joints of the 2nd and 3rd fingers which bind finger and hand. While doing this, while slightly turning your right hand from side to side, open your left hand *gradually* and *gently,* as much as can be done without inflicting an undue strain on the right hand. (Fig. 1 and 2). Repeat this between the 3rd and 4th, 4th and 5th, 2nd and 4th, 2nd and 5th, 3rd and 5th, 1st (thumb) and 2nd, 1st and 3rd of right hand. Fig. 3 to 12).

Fig. 1

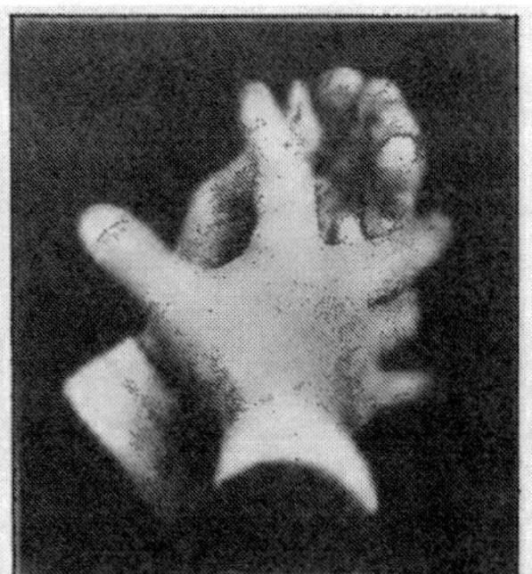
Fig. 2

Fig. 3

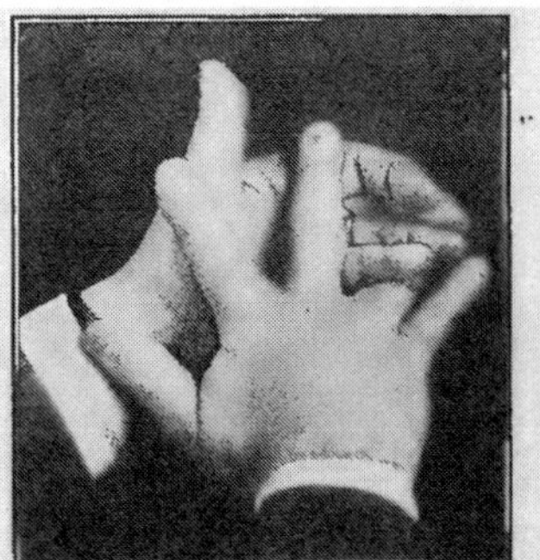
Fig. 4

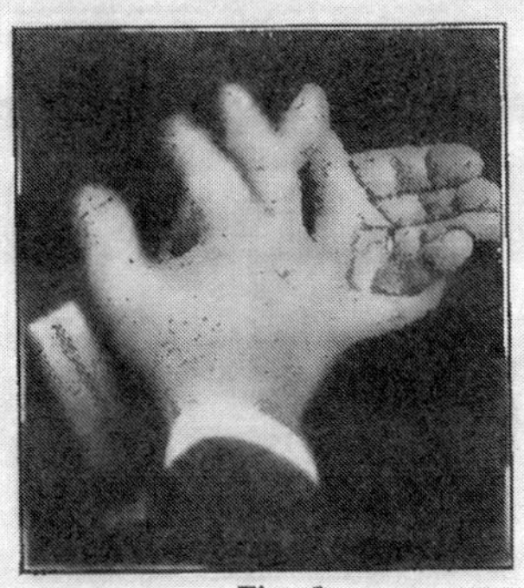
Fig. 5

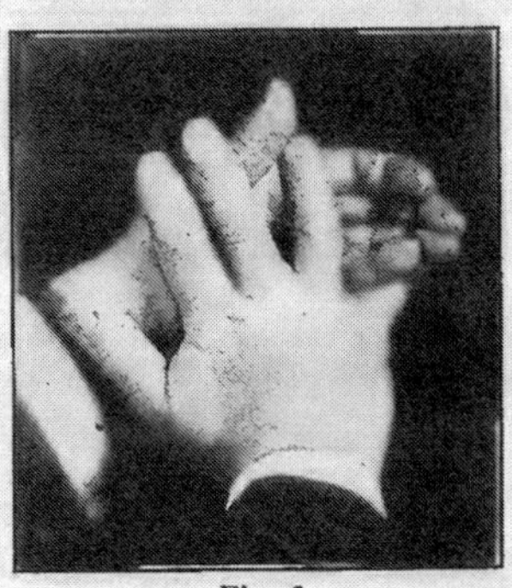
Fig. 6

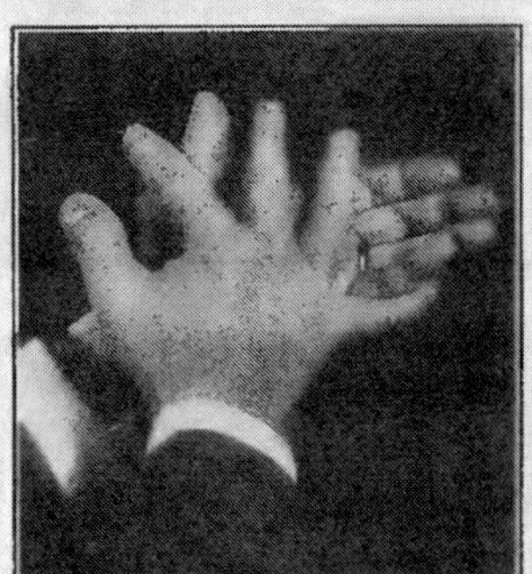
Fig. 7

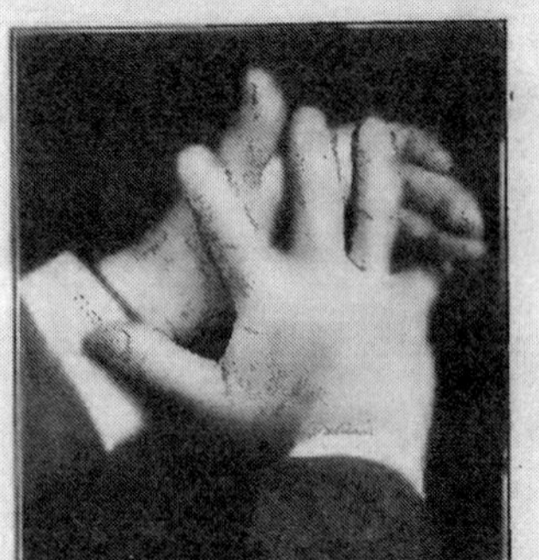
Fig. 8

EXERCISES FOR FINGERS WRISTS AND ARMS AWAY FROM THE PIANO

Exercises for Fingers, Wrists and Arms Away from the Piano

IT has always been the hope of every aspiring pianist to discover some gymnastic exercises, away from the piano, that would so strengthen his fingers, hands and arms and render them so supple as not to make it necessary for him to practise technical exercises on the piano. Let it be said at the outset that such a hope can never be fulfilled. Nothing can replace work accomplished at the keyboard.

The flexibility and strength which are required when playing the piano are *sui generis,* that is to say, peculiar to the nature, resources and demands of that instrument; these requirements (strength and flexibility) are different in quality on other musical instruments.

Still, it cannot be gainsaid that there are a few gymnastic exercises which, if indulged in with moderation and intelligence, will make the hand flexible and strong in a way that is helpful for the acquisition of a pianistic technic.

The object of many of these gymnastic exercises accomplished away from the piano consists in increasing the stretch between the fingers and the reach of the hand (from thumb to fifth finger). In order to obtain these results, most pianists pull their fingers apart and press their hand, opened wide, firmly against a table or any other hard surface. It may be asserted, however, that very little good is to be derived from these proceedings and that they are likely to do harm by weakening the ligaments and tendons of the hand.

These ligaments, which bind the fingers to each other, should not be stretched unduly, lest their contracting power becomes affected. Simply "pulling" the fingers apart is apt to bring about this deplorable result. Besides, while endeavoring to stretch the fingers in the manner described, the ligaments remain *passive* and the momentary gain in stretch is followed by a greater contraction of the ligaments and by stiffness and fatigue of the joints.

Quite dangerous and harmful is the practice of inserting pieces of cork or of felt between the fingers. The various stretching machines which have been devised are also dangerous and do more harm than good.

The example of Robert Schumann who crippled his hand permanently in his endeavor to make the fourth finger of his right hand more flexible by violent means will ever remain a warning.

It would seem unnecessary to say that a surgical operation—cutting the skin between the fingers—should not for a moment be given serious thought, were it not that I have found many persons who believe that such an operation would increase the stretch between their fingers. Of all harmful devices it is the very worst.

Stretching Exercises

The following hand gymnastics, done away from the piano, I believe the best for increasing the stretch of the hand and also the stretch between the fingers. They promote flexibility of the ligaments and tendons and benefit the hand in a general way.

Bring the thumb of your left hand in contact with the tip of the 5th finger of the same hand. Place them both, thumb and fifth finger, between the second and third finger of your right hand, half-way between the tip and the root of the fingers. Now turn slightly your right hand from side to side, in such a way that the hand "gives" at the joints of the 2nd and 3rd fingers which bind finger and hand. While doing this, while slightly turning your right hand from side to side, open your left hand *gradually* and *gently*, as much as can be done without inflicting an undue strain on the right hand. (Fig. 1 and 2). Repeat this between the 3rd and 4th, 4th and 5th, 2nd and 4th, 2nd and 5th, 3rd and 5th, 1st (thumb) and 2nd, 1st and 3rd of right hand. Fig. 3 to 12).

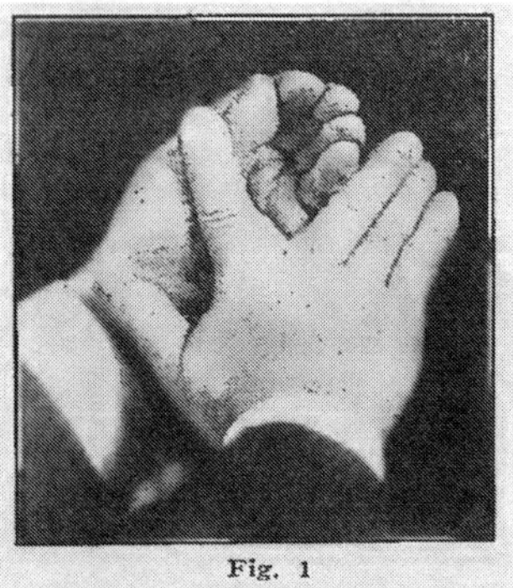

Fig. 1

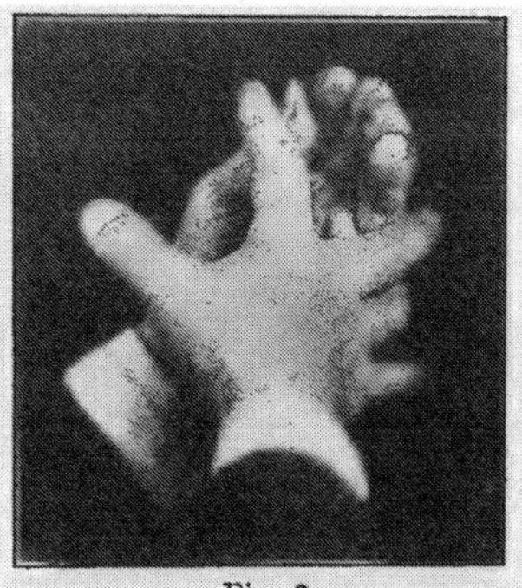

Fig. 2

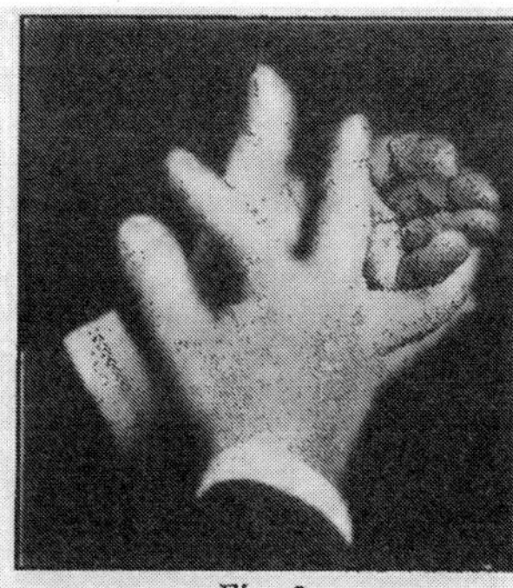

Fig. 3

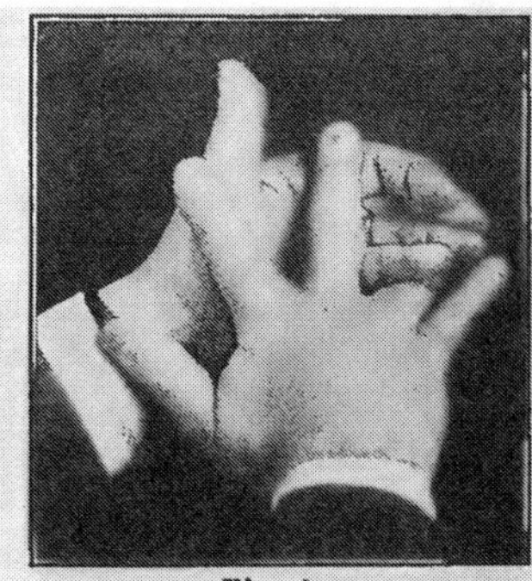

Fig. 4

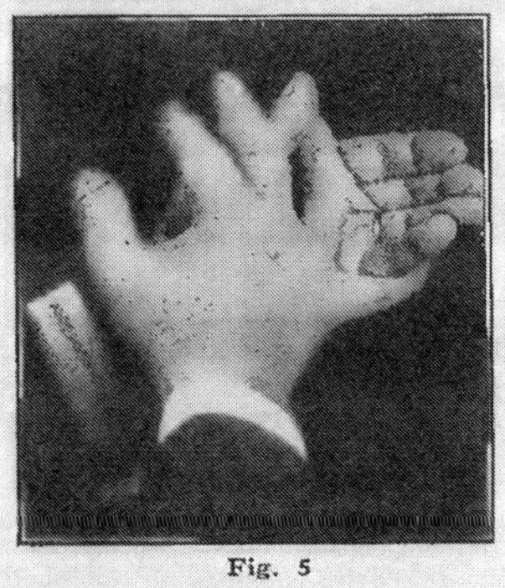

Fig. 5

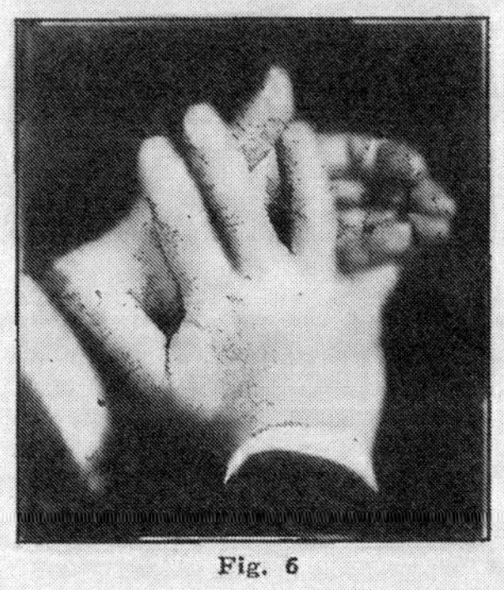

Fig. 6

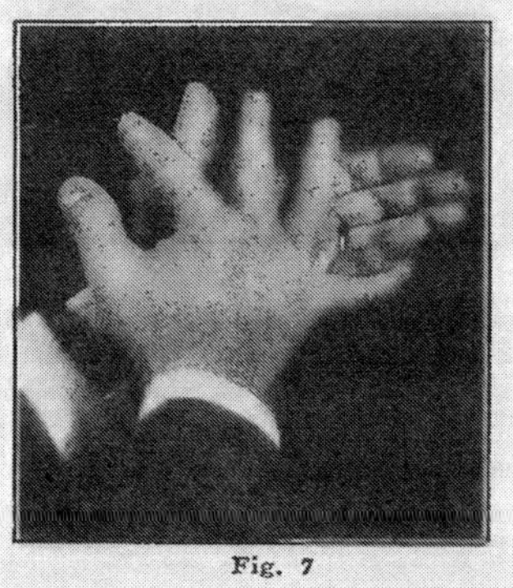

Fig. 7

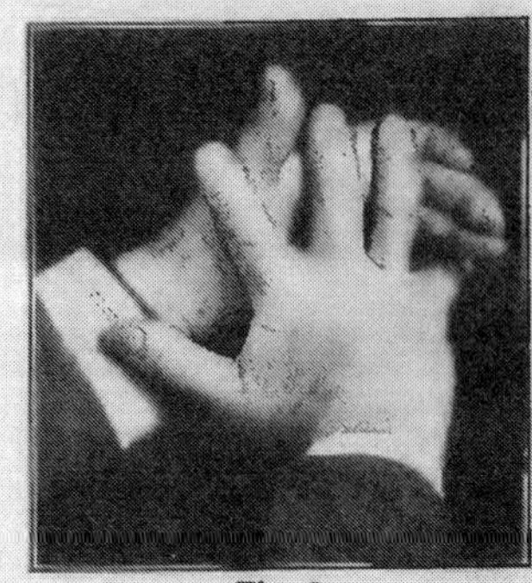

Fig. 8

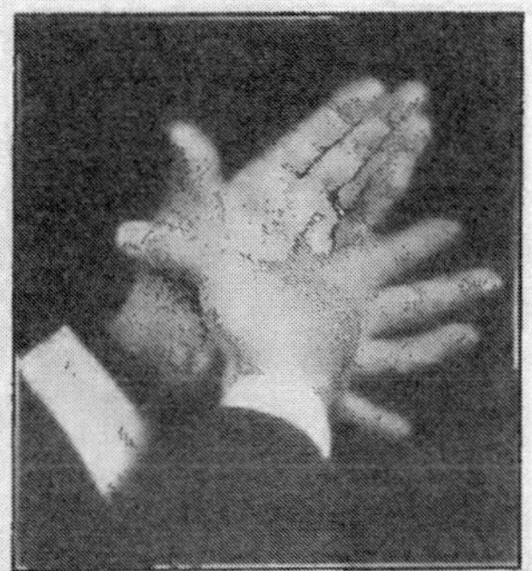

Fig. 9

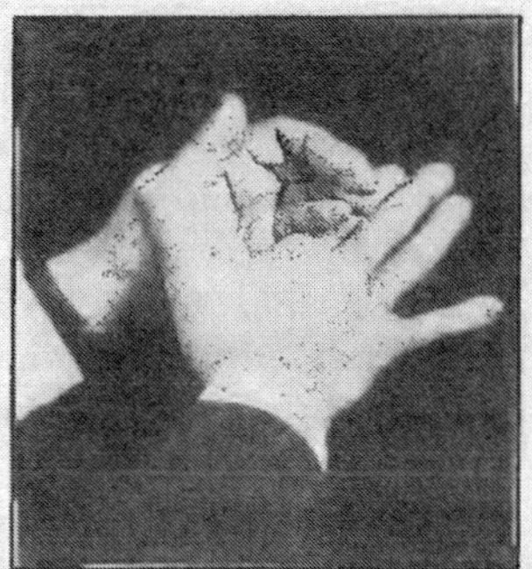

Fig. 10

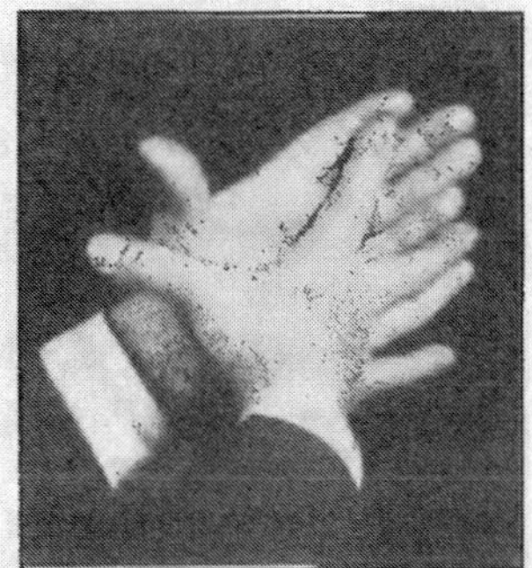

Fig. 11

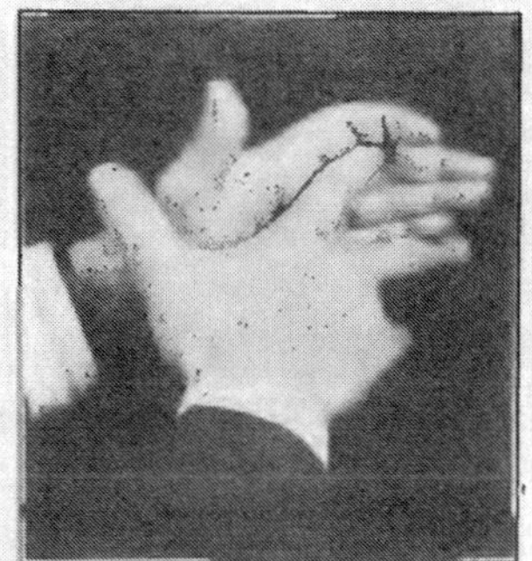

Fig. 12

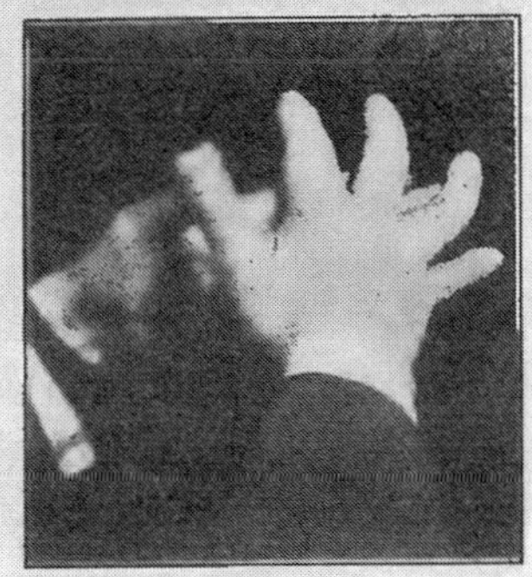

Fig. 13

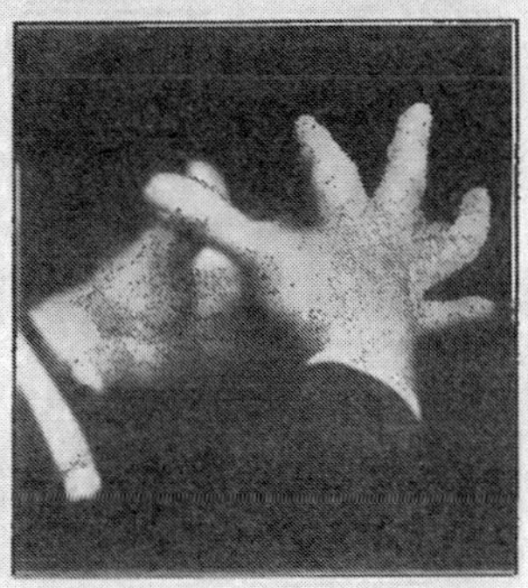

Fig. 14

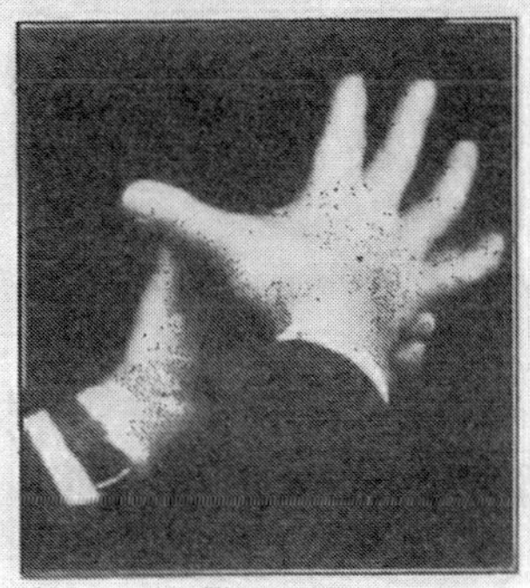

Fig. 15

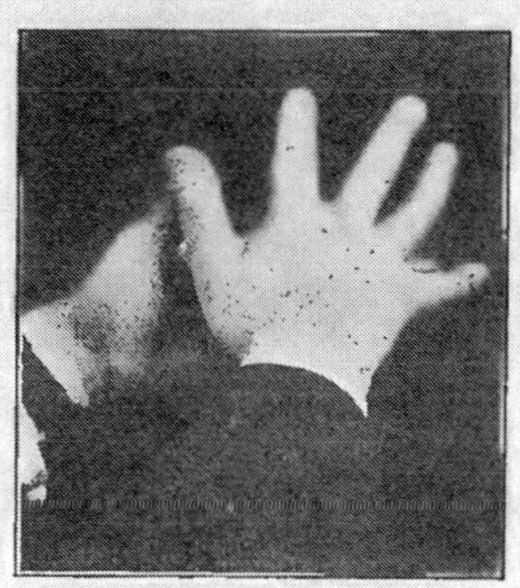

Fig. 16

When done between the thumb and 4th and between the thumb and 5th, place the left thumb against the right thumb (a little below the tip and slightly sideways) and the third left finger against the middle of the 4th or of the 5th of right hand. Turn very slightly the right hand, from side to side, while the left hand stretches it gently. (Fig. 13, 14, 15, 16).

The result of these manipulations is that while the left hand stretches the ligaments between the fingers of the right hand, these ligaments are *actively* exercised through the side-to-side motion of the right hand.

Reverse proceedings for the stretching of the ligaments between the fingers of the left hand.

These exercises are decidedly helpful not only in increasing stretch and reach of the fingers, but also in promoting the flexibility and strength of the ligaments and tendons. They will help to make your hands "fit" and active.

Weak Finger Joints

A common defect of piano students is to play with "caved in" finger joints, especially the joint nearest the end of the finger. The result is a weak, uneven touch, unevenness of tone, increasing weakness of the joint and an unsightly position of the fingers.

In order to overcome the bad habit of "caving in" the finger joints, unceasing vigilance and painstaking care in keeping a good finger position *while playing the piano* are necessary. The following exercises, away from the piano, greatly help to strengthen those weak joints.

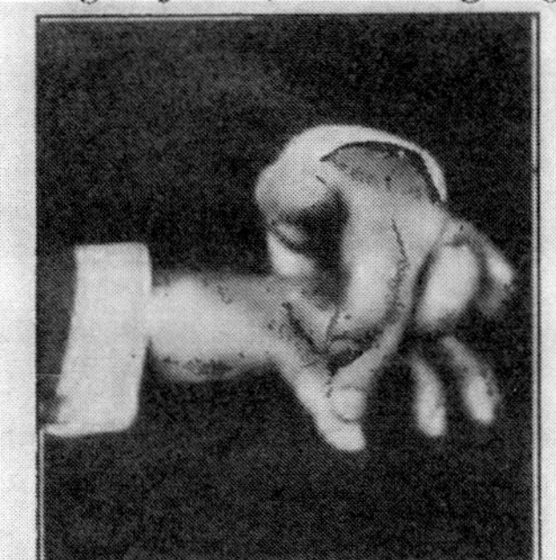

Fig. 17

Place the fingers of the right hand on a table, holding it as in a "fixed position" exercise, that is to say, the fingers slightly curved, the knuckles a little higher than the back of the hand, the wrist on a level with the table. Now press the third finger of the left hand against the last joint (nearest the tip of the finger) of the fifth finger of the right hand. While pressing with the left finger, first gently, then with increasing firmness, the fifth finger of the right hand should offer resistance at the joint which is being pressed upon (Fig. 17). It is remarkable how quickly (within a minute!) the joint which at first is easily pressed in by the other hand acquires sufficient resistance to withstand an extremely firm pressure. Do this for all three joints of every finger of the right hand. Reverse proceedings, for the strengthening of the weak joints of the left hand. This exercise can be done by placing the hand on one's knee.

Another exercise which greatly strengthens the last finger joints is the following: open the right hand well, separating the fingers as much as possible. Now bend the four fingers in such a way that the finger-tips touch the base of the fingers, that is to say, where the fingers join the hand; the end of the thumb is to be bent as in the illustration. (Fig. 18, 19). Keep the fingers in this position for a moment, then open the hand again fully. Repeat ten times, gradually faster. Do this also with the left hand. Finally, practice both hands at the same time. (A somewhat similar, but in my opinion less effective exercise is to be found in E. Ward Jackson's "Gymnastics for the Fingers and Wrist.")

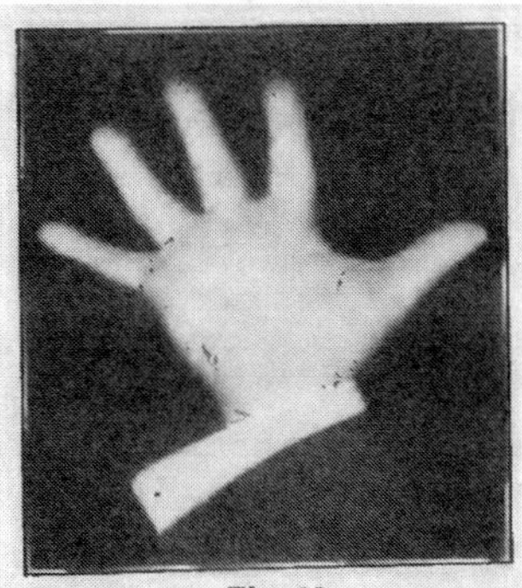

Fig. 18

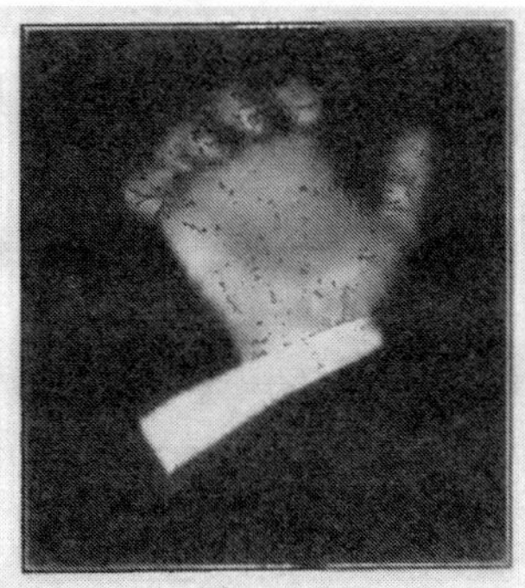

Fig. 19

Exercises for the Thumbs

(See pages 4, 5 and 6 for illustrations)

No. 1. Open the right hand wide, the fingers held wide apart (Fig. 20); then bring the end of the thumb into contact with the tip of the fifth finger (Fig. 21); again open the hand wide (Fig. 20) and place, this time, the end of the thumb on the base of the fifth finger (Fig. 22). Repeat the whole proceeding ten times. Do this likewise with the left hand. Finally with both hands together.

This exercise is to be done also by touching, with the end of the thumb, alternately the tip and the base of the 4th, of the 3rd, and of the 2nd fingers. (Fig. 20, 23, 20, 24, 20—20, 25, 20, 26, 20,—20, 27, 20, 28). In these two last cases, the end of the thumb rests sideways on the base of the 3rd and of the 2nd fingers.

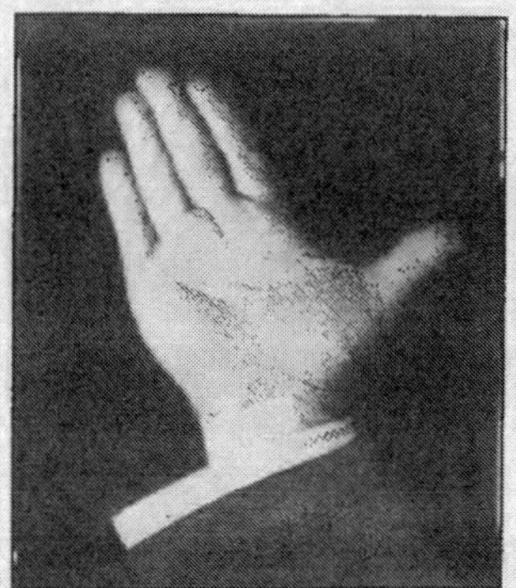

Fig. 29

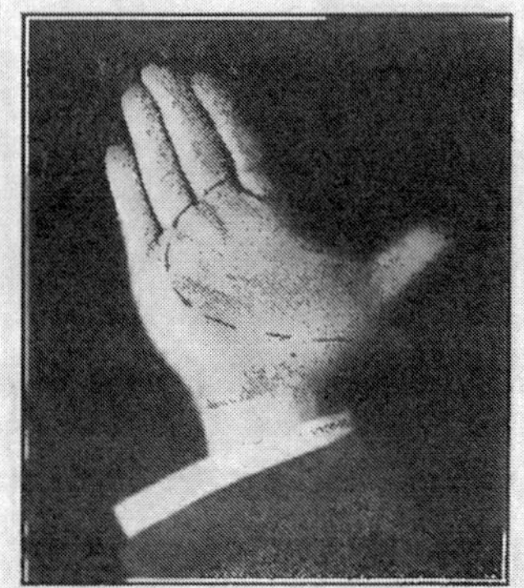

Fig. 30

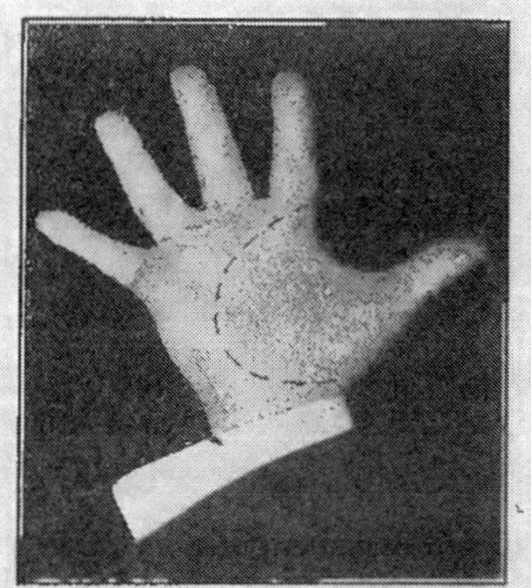

Fig. 31

No. 2. Open the right hand fully, the straightened fingers touching each other. (Fig. 29). Perform now a rotary motion of the thumb, ten times one way and ten times in the opposite direction. (Fig. 30). Repeat these two rotary movements while the fingers are held wide apart. (Fig. 31). Practice thus with the left hand; finally with both hands at the same time.

Exercises for the Wrists

For strengthening of the wrists, rotary movements of the hand, in both directions, are good, especially when the arms are extended and contracted alternately, while the hands accomplish the rotary movements.

Exercise for Stretching the Muscles

After prolonged practice the muscles are apt to get tired, and may even become strained. It is advisable to relieve the fatigue through exercises that will stretch them. The following exercise accomplishes this result: stand up straight and extend your arms behind you, the palms of the hands being turned up. Now slowly turn your arms (keeping them behind you) while stretching them gently and gradually to their full length; at the same time expand your chest, as if in the act of yawning and stretching yourself. Relax all muscles suddenly, allowing your arms to fall limp at your sides. Repeat these movements several times.

Exercise for Counteracting Round Shoulders

There are, I believe, few piano teachers who have not had to tell over and over again to their pupils to "sit straight" at the piano.

It is hardly necessary to dwell upon the evils which result from slouching, partially collapsed, attitude of the body when a person is sitting down. Rounded shoulders and a sunken, weak chest are the inevitable results. It may mean, in after-years, pulmonary trouble; it will shorten one's life.

For the pianist it means, besides, an unsightly attitude at the piano, more pronounced yet and more painful to behold in women than in men, since one naturally expects from them a more graceful carriage of the body.

The following, extremely simple, exercise, will positively prevent—in some cases even cure—round shoulders:

Stand erect and place the back of both hands against the hollow of your back, (that is to say, at the waist line), your right hand clasping your left wrist; bring out the chest. That is all. You need effect no exertion with either hands or arms, and you may in this manner walk about the room, if you so wish. Repeat this exercise while sitting down. The position just described brings out and expands the chest fully, besides giving an inward curve to the back at the waist line. A few minutes, morning, afternoon and evening, devoted to this exercise, which demands no apparatus and no special exertion, will prove of inestimable benefit to anybody, but especially to pianists, who, because of the many hours spent daily at the piano, are apt to contract the harmful habit of sitting in a slouchy position.

All the exercises described in this chapter are beneficial. But one should not forget that by themselves they do not develop pianistic technic. I recommend anew to use them sparingly and intelligently, as an aid to the daily work accomplished on the keyboard.

EXERCISES FOR THE THUMBS

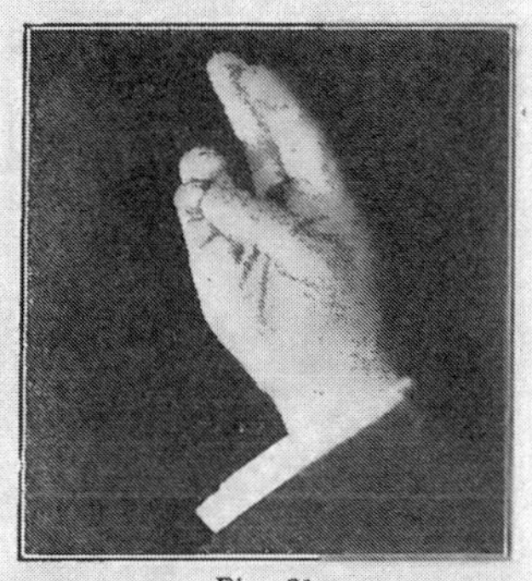

Fig. 21

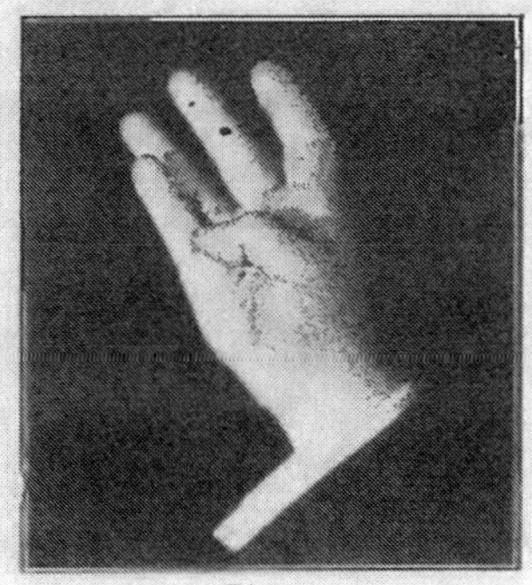

Fig. 22

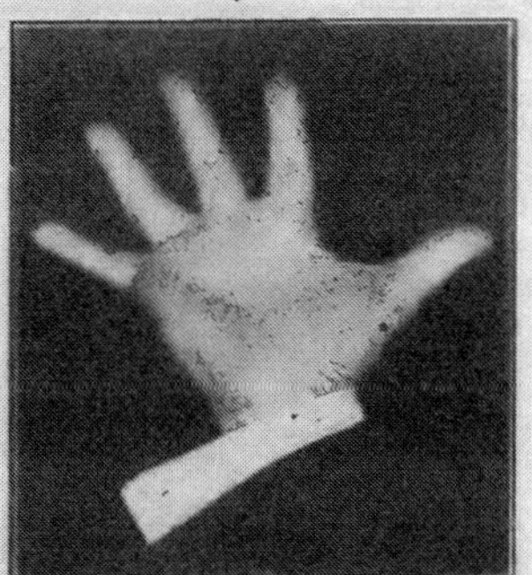

Fig. 20

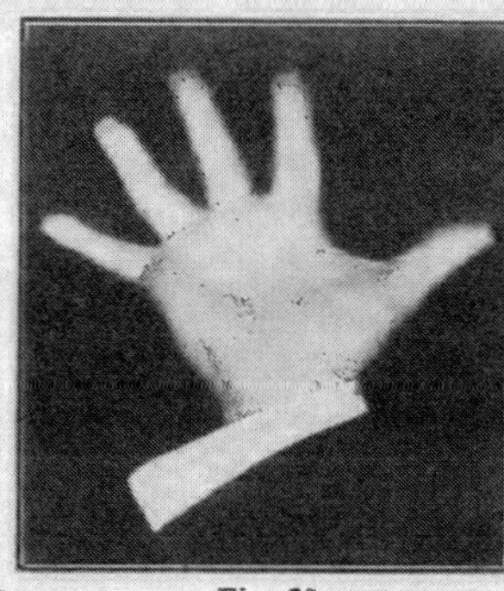

Fig. 20

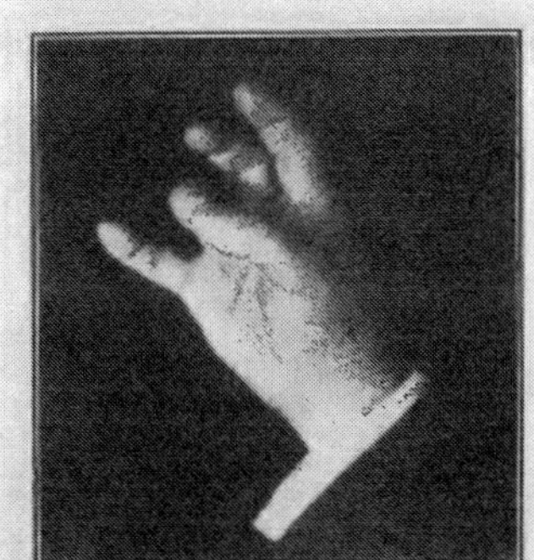

Fig. 23

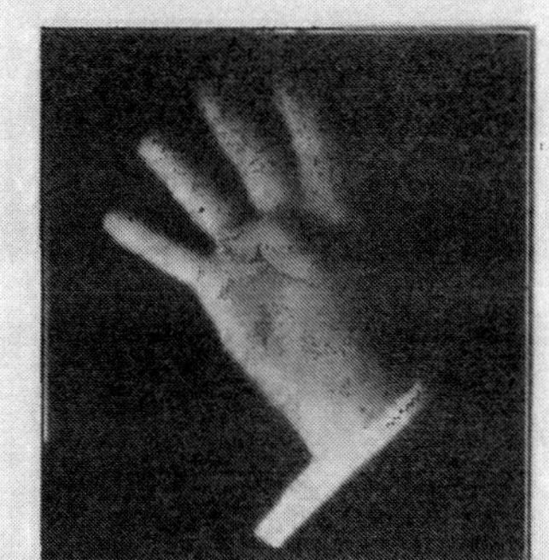

Fig. 24

EXERCISES FOR THE THUMBS

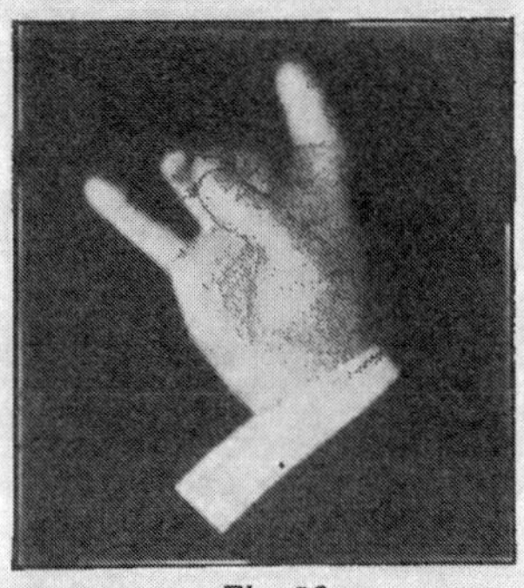

Fig. 25

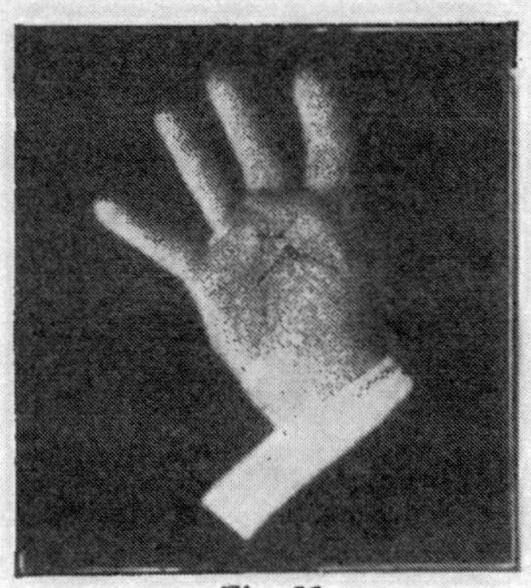

Fig. 26

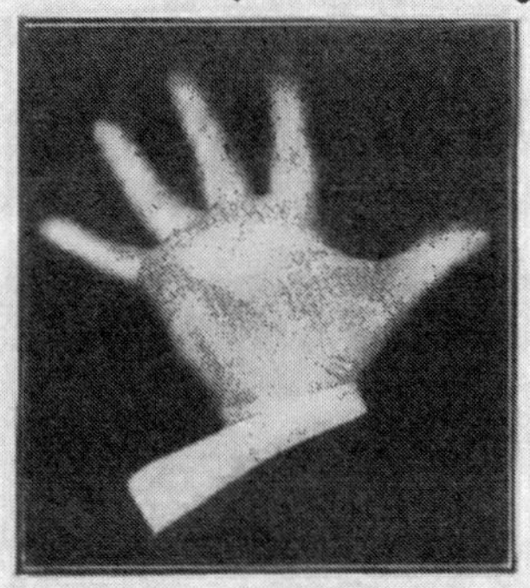

Fig. 20

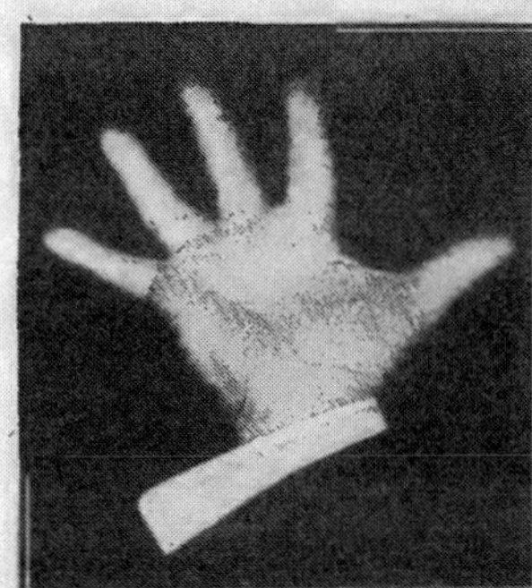

Fig. 20

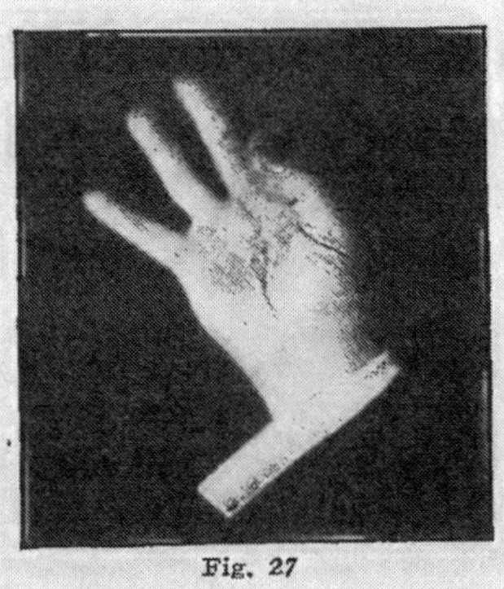

Fig. 27

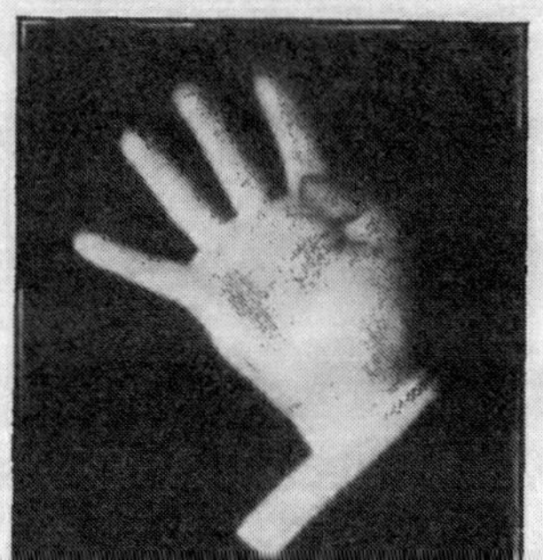

Fig. 28

Phrasing

Phrasing

Phrasing is musical punctuation, the division of a composition into sections, phrases and periods, similarly as commas, semicolons and periods are used in any language.

In language, the words which are enclosed between commas may or may not convey to us a meaning in relation to the whole sentence; likewise in music the grouping of two or more notes that follow each other may or may not give us an understanding of the musical thought. Therefore, just as when speaking and especially when reading aloud, we should delay longer on semicolons than on commas and longer on periods than on semicolons (besides laying stress on certain words because of their special importance), so should we observe the small, large and still larger subdivisions that appear in music, besides emphasizing such notes that require special rhythmical, metrical and declamatory accents. (See the chapter on "Rhythm, Measure, Accents".)

So far the simile appears to have been aptly chosen; there is, however, this distinction to be made: in language, commas and periods cannot be placed as fancy and taste dictate, but are subject to the rules of grammar, and these rules are not the same in all languages; any deviation from these rules may make the sentence unintelligible or even grotesque.

In music more latitude is allowable and it is possible to phrase --- that is to say, to subdivide --- a melody in various ways. Why this difference? Because, whereas the genius of a language and its inherent peculiarities --- such as the prevalence of idiomatic construction in English --- influence the distribution of these subdivisions of the sentence, in music we are free from such fetters.

Grove gives the following apt definition of phrasing:

"A musical composition consists of a series of short sections of various lengths, called *phrases*, each more or less complete in itself; and it is upon the interdependence of these phrases and upon their connection with each other, that the intelligibility of music depends. The phrases are analogous to the sentences of a literary composition.

"Just as the intelligent reading of a literary composition depends chiefly upon two things, accentuation and punctuation, so does musical phrasing depend on the relative strength of the sounds, and upon their connection with or separation from each other. It is this close relationship of language to music which makes their union in vocal music possible and appropriate, and accordingly when music is allied to words it is necessary that the musical accents should coincide with those of the text, while the separation of the various phrases agrees with the division of the text into separate lines or sentences. In instrumental music, although the same principles underlie its construction, there is no such definite guide as that afforded by the sense of the words in a song, and the phrasing must therefore be the result of a just appreciation on the part of the performer of the general sense of the music, and of the observance of certain marks by which phrasing is indicated."

First Mention of Phrasing in Music

No signs of phrasing are found in the manuscripts and in the early editions of the compositions by Bach, Händel, Rameau and Scarlatti. In the Well Tempered Clavichord, Bach, in isolated instances, drew a ⌒ to group two, and sometimes three notes.

Prelude in C♯ Minor, 1st Book
JOHANN SEBASTIAN BACH

Ex. 1 Andante espressivo (♩ = 76-92)

Fugue in E Minor, 1st Book
JOHANN SEBASTIAN BACH

Ex. 2 Allegro (♩ = 112-132)

Prelude in A♭ Major, 2nd Book
JOHANN SEBASTIAN BACH

Ex.3

Andante (♩ = 69 – 76)

Fugue in B Minor, 1st Book
JOHANN SEBASTIAN BACH

Ex.4

Largo (♩ = 46–56) (The tempo indication is by Bach)

The slurs in the last example might be construed as signs of phrasing; they may also have been meant as a sign for legato.

As far as is known to me, the first mention of phrasing in music appears in Jean-Jacques Rousseau's "Dictionnaire de Musique" (1767) in the chapter entitled "Ponctuer" (To Punctuate or Punctuation). He wrote, "In terms of composition, 'to punctuate' means to mark the more or less complete rests and to divide the phrases in such a manner that one feels, through the modulation and the cadences, their beginnings, endings and their greater or lesser interrelation, just as all this is felt in language, through punctuation." Rousseau says also, "The singer who feels what he sings and duly marks the phrases and accents is a man of taste."

Rousseau limits himself to the advice to divide clearly the large or smaller sections of melody. He gives no help for elucidating the problem of phrasing in an appropriate manner.

The first study of this subject appeared in an article entitled "Vortrag" (Execution) by Joh. Abr. Peter Schulz, included in Sulzer's "Theorie der schönen Künste" (1772). It is so explicit and interesting that I reproduce it here.

"The beginnings of phrases correspond to the signs of punctuation in language, which must be felt through a slight pause. In music, this is accomplished by shortening the last note of a phrase and by laying a slight stress on the first note of the following phrase; but one can also diminish the intensity of the last tone and increase that of the first tone of the following phrase."

"If the phrase ends with a rest there is no difficulty in phrasing correctly, the end of the phrase and the beginning of the next being thereby indicated. But if the phrase ends without a rest it requires more skill to mark correctly the entrance of the next phrase because it is more difficult to discover it. A singer experiences no difficulty in phrasing correctly, because he must guide himself mainly by the words. Not so with the instrumentalist."

Schulz offers then the following musical examples, giving as a fundamental rule the advice to "guide oneself by the beginning of a piece", by which advice he means that the way a group of notes is played at the outset should be adhered to later, whenever that group of notes occurs again. He gives ths sign + to indicate the beginning of a phrase and O to indicate the end of the phrase.

Ex.5

Schulz then recommends the practice, already in vogue at that time, of separating the groups of notes by the manner of writing.

Ex. 6

Schulz, commenting on this mode of writing, says that it makes the phrasing very clear and should be used in preference to the customary manner. He points out, though, that it cannot be used for quarter-notes and half-notes, in which case a comma is to be employed.

Further quotations from Schulz which deserve to be made are the following:-

"It is incredible how a melody may be distorted and made unrecognizable if the entrances of phrases are not marked correctly or not marked at all. To be convinced of this, one has only to hear a gavotte performed in such manner that the entrance of the phrase in the middle of the measure is not observed. Easy as it is to understand this dance, it will thus be rendered incomprehensible."

In the following example, if the phrasing is observed, the melody is acceptable; but if one accents only the beginning of every measure, then the melody becomes very insipid.

Ex. 7

Signs to Indicate the Phrasing

As far back as 1789, Türk, in his "Klavierschule" explains that, just as in speech, the meaning of a sentence may be obscured or changed entirely through faulty punctuation, so a musical idea may be distorted by faulty phrasing. He advocated placing the sign // over the staff in order to show the divisions. This sign has been retained to this day by many musicians. Riemann uses it in his "Vademecum der Phrasierung"; Busoni, in his piano transcriptions of the Chorales of Bach.

In his lucid and instructive Preface, appended to his edition of the C major Concerto of Beethoven, Franz Kullak writes; "Nowadays the comma, just as in language, is used for the purpose of phrasing by many musicians." This was written in 1881. Kullak writes further: "This sign, as an indication when to lift the finger from the key, is of undoubted usefulness. But music has its own signs of punctuation, such as rests, holds, signs of staccato and *slurs*. It is only the slur that often gives trouble to both the performer and the editor. As can be seen by the following examples, with Beethoven the end of a ⁀ is not always a sign for lifting the hand, that is to say, it is not identical with a musical comma. The second theme of the C minor Concerto, according to the original edition (and to ours) is phrased, at its first appearance, thus:-

Ex. 8

"But who would seriously want to separate these two measures! If no slurs were given, there would be possible only one gross mistake of punctuation, supposing that anyone should want to play it thus:

Ex. 9

"He would have to be a very unmusical player! At the repetition in C major the slurs appear as follows:

Ex. 10

"It is possible that a mistake has been made and that the composer had not in mind a separation after the dotted quarter; a similar example will be found farther on. At any rate, it becomes clear that with Beethoven the *curved lines are generally to be considered as a sign of the legato.* Only in small groups, composed of two or three notes are the slurs to be regarded as positive signs for lifting the hands. For instance, in the *Adagio* of the B flat major Concerto:"

Ex.11 

The sign for the *legato*, the sign for the *tie* (connecting two notes or chords of the same pitch, the second of which is not to be played), the sign for the *slur* (connecting two notes or chords of different pitch, the second of which is to be played with the hand lifted from the keyboard), and finally the sign for *phrasing* --- all four are identical: a curved line drawn over the notes. It is easy to understand how much confusion there has always been and continues to be created by using one and the same sign for the legato and for phrasing.

We have seen that commas were used in music prior to the year 1881. There is no reason for not using also semicolons and periods, but all these punctuation marks should be placed between parenthesis over the staff. They might be used in conjunction with the old signs of Schulz (O to show the end of a phrase and + to indicate its beginning), or better yet, by └ to indicate the beginning and ┘ to indicate the end. By using these signs in conjunction with commas and semicolons, whenever required, there would be no need for curved lines over *measures and groups of measures* and there would be no confusion between the sign of the legato and the sign of phrasing, the latter representing the construction of a musical composition.

It usually takes time for an innovation to become popular. Yet, any earnest musician who is able and willing to put aside routine should give the matter careful thought. A modification of our present confusing way of using the same curved line for everything seems absolutely necessary.

What Influences and Determines the Manner of Phrasing?

Phrasing is dependent on:-

1. The manner in which the shorter divisions of a complete musical sentence, or period, begin and end, and in their structural development, that is to say, musical form.
2. The nature of the theme itself.
3. The relative value of the notes.
4. The manner in which the notes are grouped.
5. The re-appearance of the theme.
6. The accentuation and the delay on certain notes.
7. The repetition of certain melodic notes.
8. Progressions
9. Skips

* * * * * * *

1. In order to recognize the shorter divisions or phrases, we should remember the quotation from Peter Schulz, given early in this chapter: "If the phrase ends with a rest, there is no difficulty in phrasing correctly, the end of the phrase and the beginning of the next being thereby indicated."

Sonata Op. 2, No. 1
LUDWIG van BEETHOVEN

Ex.12 

Not every rest is to be regarded as ending a phrase. In the following example the 8th notes, followed by rests, may be considered as being equivalent to quarter-notes with a staccato sign:

Sonata Op. 14, No. 2
LUDWIG van BEETHOVEN

Ex.13 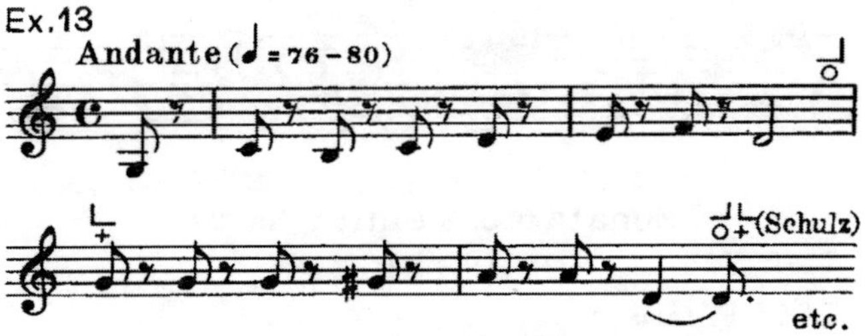

In his "Vademecum der Phrasierung" (Vademecum of Phrasing) Riemann points out that if a phrase ends with a note of longer value, on which repose is due, the separation between that phrase and the next is also made self-evident. The musical examples given by Riemann are many and convincing. Suffice it to reproduce the following:

Sonata Op.110
LUDWIG van BEETHOVEN

Ex.14
Allegro molto (𝅗𝅥 = 126-138)

Sonata Op.42
FRANZ SCHUBERT

Ex.15
Moderato (𝅗𝅥 = 96-104)

A third consideration regarding the ending of the shorter divisions, is apt to determine the manner of phrasing. If a phrase or a period terminates with a single note on the first beat of the measure, or with a note on the first beat followed by another on the third beat (in 4/4 time) it is said to have a "masculine", or "strong" ending; when this final note melts into, or is followed by, one or more notes on the so-called weak beats (second beat in duple and second and third beats in triple and in quadruple time), it is said to have a "feminine", or "weak" ending, in analogy to verse.

Sonata Op. 2, No.2
LUDWIG van BEETHOVEN

Ex.16
Allegro vivace (♩=132-144)

Sonata (Cotta edition No. 3)
JOSEPH HAYDN

Ex.17 Presto

As to the structural development of the theme, there can be no doubt that a knowledge of musical form will enable the student to phrase more correctly than if he possesses none.

The words *theme, subject* and *motive* have been used often by didactic writers, and also by great composers, without a specification as to their different meanings. What is a theme, a subject and a motive? Are they synonymous or of different nature?

Says Grove: "Subject is the theme, or leading idea, on which a musical composition is based. A piece of music can no more be composed without a subject than a sermon can be preached without a text. Rich harmonies and graceful passages may be strung together in any number; but if they be not suggested by a leading thought, they will mean nothing. The "leading thought" is the subject; and the merit of the composition based upon that subject will depend, in the first place, upon the worthiness of the idea, and in the second, upon the skill with which the composer discourses upon it....." Grove goes on to say that the term "is to be applied in its fullest significance to the principal subject of a musical composition, although in general language it is frequently used to denote a subject of any kind, whether of a leading or subsidiary character. From the time of Sebastian Bach to our own, the terms 'theme' and 'subject' have been used with much looseness. In his 'Musikalisches Opfer' Bach designates the motive given to him by Frederick the Great as 'Il Soggetto Réale', in one place, and 'Thema regium' in another; thus proving conclusively that he considered the two terms as interchangeable. But in another work founded on a motive by Legrenzi, he calls the principal subject 'Thema', and the counter-subject 'Subjectum', and this is unquestionably the more correct method of using the terms."

If I add that some musical writers consider the word "motif" or "motive" as representing the notes contained in one single measure (see Niecks, "Dictionary of Musical Terms"), while the majority use it in the same sense as theme and as subject, the conclusion is reached that the three terms are synonymous.

A musical theme may begin on any of the beats

of a measure; on the second, third and fourth, not necessarily on the first.

If the theme comprises one measure, let it be remembered that this measure may be counted, not only from first beat to first beat, but also from second to second, from third to third, etc. Thus the up-beat before the bar and the next down-beat after the bar count for one measure of $^2/_4$ time.

A musical *sentence* or *period* may be composed of any number of measures, but in its simpler, most usual form it consists of eight measures. This period is divided into two "phrases", of four measures each. The first half is called by many English musicians the *antecedent*, or *proposition*; the second half is called the *consequent*, or *answer*. Each phrase is divided into two *sections* of two measures each. Each section may be divided further into single measures and these single measures into half-measures. To summarize: period (8), phrase (4), section (2), measure (1).

A period alone, although in itself a complete musical sentence, seldom affords scope for contrast, which is one of the four essentials in music (the other three are motion, repose and symmetry). Therefore, a still larger form is sometimes resorted to, a double-period, and usually the second of these two periods brings the desired contrast.

Sonata Op.10, No 1

LUDWIG van BEETHOVEN

Ex.18

Prestissimo ($\sharp$ = 100 - 126)

If a theme covers two measures, the normal manner of proceeding is: two, two and four measures. Or two, two, four and eight measures.

Sonata Op.90

LUDWIG van BEETHOVEN

Ex.19

Animato e sempre con espressione

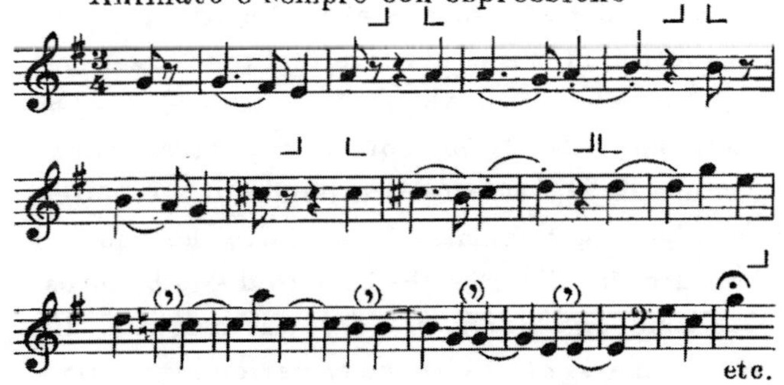

If every piece of music were constructed according to these metrical divisions, a dire monotony would be the result. Therefore, while the structure of periods is generally symmetrical, consisting of an even number of measures (four and four, or three and three, etc.) yet we also find some periods composed of four and three, four and five, two and three, etc. In some cases the last measure of a period is also the first measure of the following period. In short, it is, at times, not easy (although it is always possible) to distinguish clearly the beginnings and endings of phrases and sections.

Bars

Bars have been introduced into musical annotation in order to facilitate reading by dividing the measures. They always occur at the end of a measure and before the so-called strong beat of the following measure. But we have seen that a theme may begin and also end on other beats than the first; consequently, the phrasing of a musical composition should be dependent not on the distribution of the bars, but on the theme only.

Some composers (none less than Chopin, Schumann and Liszt) have at times misplaced these bars, which circumstance is, of course, not calculated to make the task easier for the student of musical form. Thus, the "Eglogue", and also the Finale of the A major Concerto, both by Liszt, were written in 4/4 time. The correct time is 2/2, or ₵, and thus have these compositions been published in subsequent, revised editions.

Chopin's well-known Nocturne in E flat major is written in 12/8. Riemann in his Catechism of Piano Playing" very justly points out that the correct time is 6/8.

Schumann has also mistaken the true period-construction of one of his loveliest tone-creations, the well-known "Des Abends" (Fantasy Pieces, Op. 12) written in 3/8. In my opinion the correct time-signature is 6/16, which corresponds to the note-value given by Schumann, or 6/8 if one chooses to substitute 8th notes in the bass to the 16th notes. These time-signatures preserve the original division of the whole sentence or period into sixteen measures, of which the last eight form the natural "consequent" to the first eight, which represent the "antecedent". By adopting 6/8 or 6/16 the difficulty generally experienced in the blending of the two different rhythms (which difficulty led Otto Neitzel to publish this piece with 3/8 for the right hand and 2/8 for the left hand) disappears entirely. Both rhythms appear then in their logical relation to each other, and while the piece becomes easier to play, it loses none of the charm which the two different rhythms imparts to this lovely tone-poem.

Fantasy Pieces, Op.12, No.1

ROBERT SCHUMANN

Ex. 20

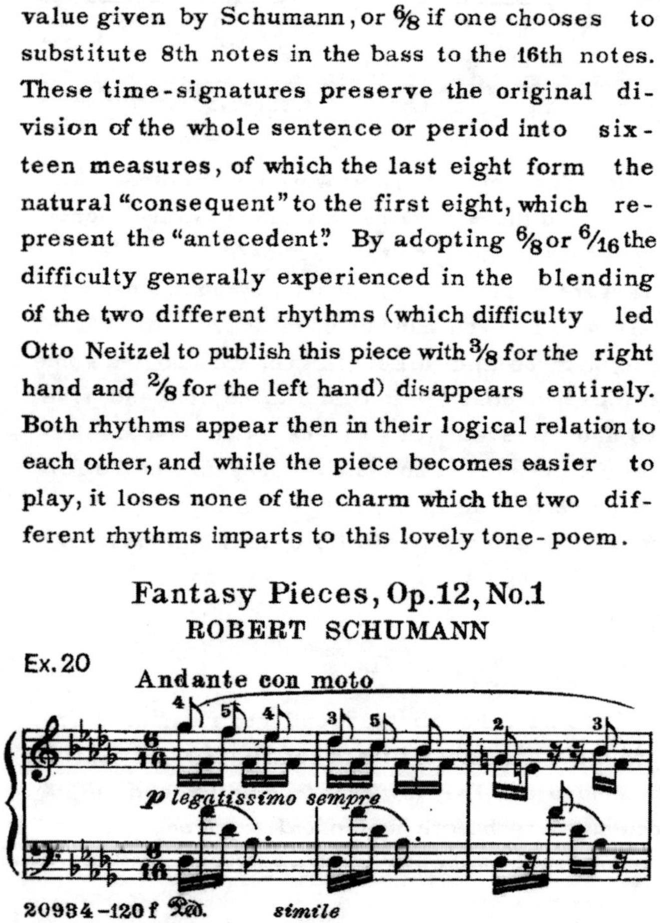

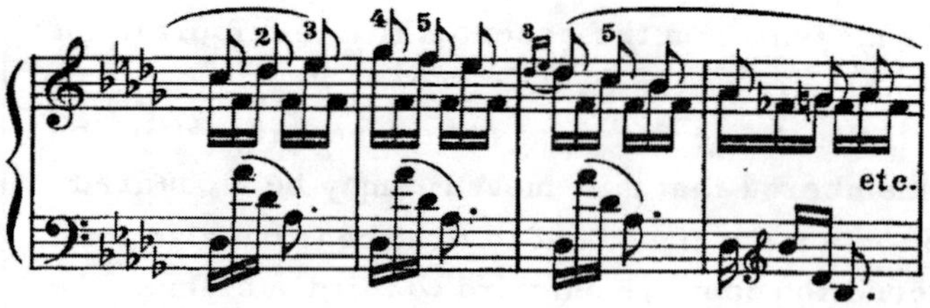

2. A theme of a passionate, throbbing character usually requires short, vehement phrases:-

Sonata Op. 57

LUDWIG van BEETHOVEN

Ex. 21

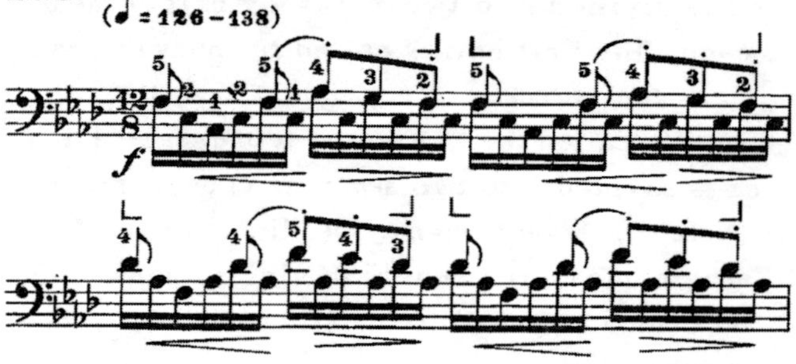

There are exceptions, though:-

Scherzo in B♭ Minor

FREDERICK CHOPIN

Ex. 22

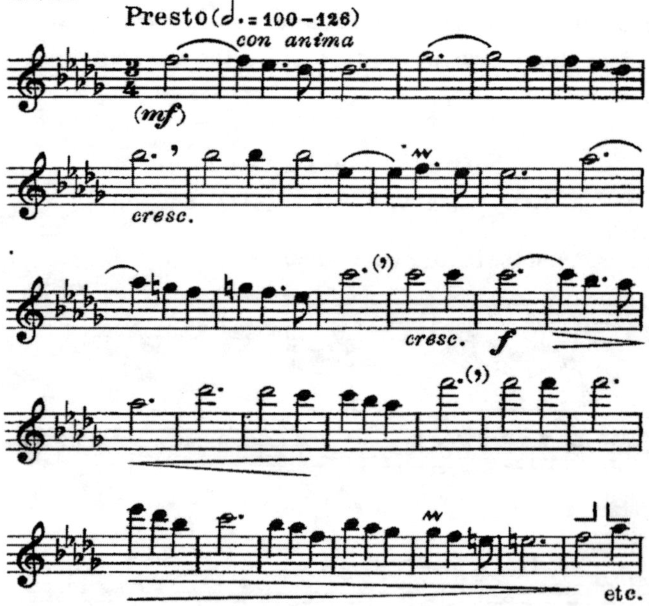

But when the theme is of a broad, tranquil character, the phrasing is seldom, if ever, short-lived; it follows the breadth and mirrors the serenity of the theme.

Sonata, Op. 5
JOHANNES BRAHMS

Ex. 23

Andante espressivo

3. A division of the phrase occurs often after a note of longer time-value than the notes which precede or which follow it:-

Sonata Op. 7
LUDWIG van BEETHOVEN

Ex. 24 Poco Allegretto e grazioso

Sonata Op. 49, No. 2
LUDWIG van BEETHOVEN

Ex. 25

Tempo di Menuetto (♩ = 112-116)

In some instances, the disconnection of the phrasing takes place after the very first note of the theme:-

Fugue in A Major, 1st Book
JOHANN SEBASTIAN BACH

Ex. 26

Moderato (♩. = 66-72)

Sonata Pathétique, Op. 13
LUDWIG van BEETHOVEN

Ex. 27 Grave (♪ = 66-69)

4. The grouping of the notes has an influence on the phrasing, because it influences the accentuation. Turns should be played in one group, or phrase, and not be subdivided (See Master School, Book III, page 196).

Unless indicated by the composer, scales (diatonic and chromatic) and arpeggios which are made up of notes of even time-value should not be subdivided, but should be played in one group or phrase. (See Master School, Book II, page 267. The six measures are to be played in one phrase).

5. As a rule the reappearance of a theme requires a new phrasing, that is to say, the hand should be lifted from the keyboard. At times this holds good even when the theme is apparently not disconnected from the preceding notes:

Sonata Op. 27, No. 1
LUDWIG van BEETHOVEN

Ex. 28

Allegro Vivace (♩ = 126-138)

Sonata in A Major
WOLFGANG AMADEUS MOZART

Ex.29 Rondo
Alla Turca
Allegretto (♩=126-138)

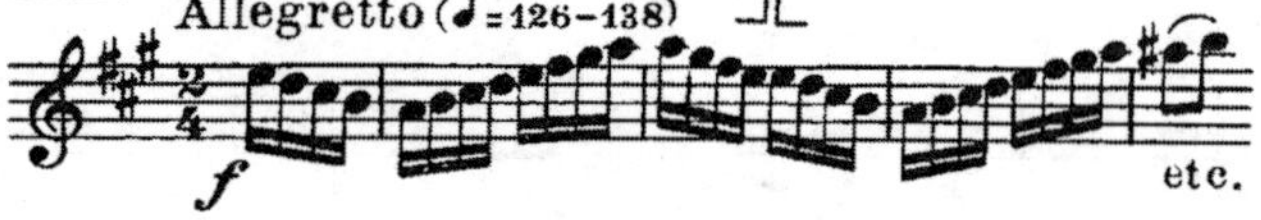

But if the re-entrance of a theme is the apex, or highest point of a diatonic or chromatic scale, there is no need for a new phrasing; the hand need not be lifted from the keyboard.

Concerto in C Minor
LUDWIG van BEETHOVEN

Ex.30 Rondo
Allegro (♩=108-120)
(legato)

6. Next to lifting the hand from the keyboard, the most effective means for phrasing are accentuation and delay. The necessity for "accents of phrasing" has already been pointed out in the chapter on "Rhythm, Measure, Accents."

The direct influence of the grouping of the notes on the accents of phrasing is justly appreciated by Grove:-

"There are certain irregular forms of accent occasionally required by the phrasing, which it is necessary to notice."

"As a rule, the accent of a passage follows the grouping, the first note of each group receiving the accent; whenever, therefore, the grouping of a passage consisting of notes of equal length varies, the number of accents in the bar must vary also." Thus in the next example the first bar will contain four accents, while the third requires but two."

Sonata Op.14, No.2
LUDWIG van BEETHOVEN

Ex.31
Allegro (♩=84-96)

A monotonous hammering of every D flat in the melody was evidently not intended by Chopin in the first theme of his B flat minor Sonata. By giving accents of phrasing, as shown in the following example, justice is done to the structural and melodic development.

Ex.32 (𝅗𝅥=108-120)

Chopin drew a curved line over the four introductory measures of his Ballade in G minor. Yet a division to show the repetition of the "motive" or theme seems absolutely necessary. It is given in the Klindworth edition. These divisions, or groupings, can be made audible without lifting the hand from the keyboard,- that is to say, by a very slight delay on the last note of the smaller phrase, or by a very slight accent on the first note of the following small phrase. This results in a second phrasing, within the larger phrasing.

Ballade in G Minor *(Klindworth edition)*
FREDERICK CHOPIN

Ex.33
Lento

7. Provided that it occurs after at least one, preferably two measures, the repetition of a note in the melody is often a sign for phrasing anew:

Sonata in C Major, No. 3
WOLFGANG AMADEUS MOZART

Ex. 34.

8. The importance of the musical design, or theme, in a progression, has already been emphasized in the chapters on "The Artistic Employment of Dynamics and Agogics" and "The Art of Memorizing". The theme itself is also a guide for phrasing correctly. At times the phrasing is to be made very obvious by lifting the hand from the keyboard:

Fantasy in F Minor
FREDERICK CHOPIN

Ex. 35

At other times the phrasing should be made apparent, not by lifting the hand, but by accents of phrasing:

Sonata Op. 26
LUDWIG van BEETHOVEN

Ex. 36

9. There is no rule without exceptions, but usually a skip indicates a new subdivision of the phrase.

Sonata Op. 22
LUDWIG van BEETHOVEN

Ex. 37

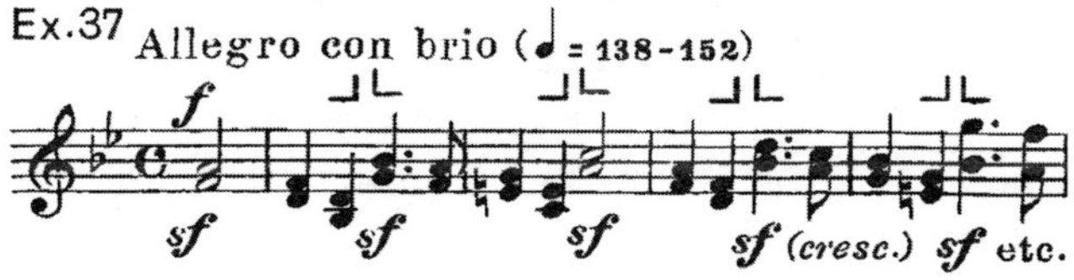

Sonata Op. 31, No. 1
LUDWIG van BEETHOVEN

Ex. 38

The Well Tempered Clavichord

On account of the several phrasings given by various editors, the Preludes and Fugues of the Well Tempered Clavichord by Bach offer the best possible examples for the study of phrasing.

In the Fugue in C major, 1st Book, the "subject" (theme) is phrased as follows in the editions of Czerny and of Tausig.

Ex. 39

A better phrasing is given in the editions of Wouters (Schott Frères) and of Busoni (Breitkopf and Haertel):

Ex. 40

This way of phrasing the theme (which appeared first in the Wouters edition and was sanctioned by Gevaert, the erudite Belgian musician) eliminates the awkward sequence of the two intervals of the fourth, and gives the proper rhythmical accent to the dominant, on the second beat, whereby a more satisfactory termination of the "subject" is obtained on the first beat.

The Prelude and Fugue in G minor of the first book, appear phrased as follows in various editions:

Prelude

Ex. 41
Czerny

Tausig

Fugue

Ex. 42
Wouters
Larghetto

Busoni
Andante con moto

Czerny
Andante con moto (♩ = 63)

The "subject" of the Fugue in C minor, first book, has been phrased variously:

Ex. 43
Bischoff
Allegretto (♩ = 80)

Wouters
Allegretto (♩ = 76)

d'Albert
Allegro moderato

Busoni
Allegretto, vivacemente

Reinecke
Allegretto moderato

Czerny
Allegretto moderato (♩ = 80)

The "subject" of the C sharp major Fugue, first book, has also been phrased in more than one way.

Ex. 44
Busoni
Allegro moderato

Tausig - d'Albert
Allegro moderato

Wouters - Bischoff

Czerny
Allegro

The "subject" of the fugue in E♭ major, second book, is phrased as follows in Czerny's edition.

Ex. 45 Allegro maestoso (♩ = 132)

A better phrasing is given in the Wouters edition:

Ex. 46 Moderato (♩ = 132)

Two and Three Part Inventions

In nearly all editions, the F major Two Part Invention, by Bach, appears phrased in this manner:

Ex. 47

Busoni, in his edition (Breitkopf and Haertel) claims the following to be correct:

Ex. 48

As a study in phrasing the Two Part Invention No. 9, in Busoni's edition, deserves special attention.

Touch and Phrasing

An error indulged in by many musicians is to confuse the phrasing with the *touch*. The length or shortness of the subdivisions of a phrase are the same whether the notes are played legato or staccato. In the following example the divisions would be the same if all the notes were to be played legato:

Rigaudon
JOSEPH JOACHIM RAFF

Ex. 49 Allegro

Conclusion

The importance of phrasing correctly must be manifest to every cultured musician. Yet it is also self-evident that it is possible to err through too much zeal in this, as in other artistic pursuits. It is therefore not amiss to contrast the profuse explanations and extended analysis of phrasing given by Riemann, Bülow and others with the following statement by Franz Kullak.

"We do not believe that there is any danger for anyone who has had a thorough musical education of phrasing insufficiently or in a faulty manner. A greater evil seems to us the modern tendency to phrase *too much*. The reason for this lies perhaps in the desire to transfer to the piano the characteristics of other instruments, such as, for example, the bowing of the violin."

In his "Catechism of Piano Playing" Riemann, referring to phrasing, makes a statement that in itself is a confession: "One will hardly miss the general outline if one calls the ear to aid, for it often, with unerring instinct, detects the truth quicker than the mind."

In every form of art there are two categories of exponents: those who can work and express themselves only through Rule, Theory and Principles; and those that allow their artistic expression to spring from and be founded on Feeling, Spontaniety and Emotion. Happy he who strives to blend harmoniously the power of his developed intellect with the natural impulse of his emotional self and with his imagination.

Embellishments

in

Music

Embellishments in Music

Embellishments, or Grace Notes are ornaments introduced into vocal and instrumental music, which are indicated by small notes or by certain signs or symbols.

At present we have in music comparatively few of these relics of the past, because of the modern custom of writing out musical ornaments in full. Modern editions of the classics should either reproduce in usual notes the old-fashioned signs, or give an explanation and illustration of how the small grace notes, signs or symbols should be performed. However, this is not always done; besides, the well educated musician should be conversant with the meaning of these old signs, not only because he must know what the great composers really wrote, but because grace notes, as well as some of the old signs, are still in general use (for example, the sign of the turn and of the arpeggiando). It is, therefore, not amiss to devote a Chapter to what Carl Philipp Emanuel Bach deemed "of the *foremost importance* in music".

According to the most authoritative musical historians, grace notes were first introduced by Chambonnières (1600-1670). He has been called the father of the Suite, and the paternity of ornaments in music is also to be attributed to him. Grace notes came quickly into general use, because they helped to cover up, or to extend and beautify, the small, thin tone, of very little duration, of the spinets (which also were called virginals) and the clavichords then in use.

Jean Jacques Rousseau, in his "Dictionnaire de Musique" (1767) refers to them as necessities-- "to cover up somewhat the insipidness of French songs."

Grace notes were then executed according to the individual caprice and impulse of the performer. The first definite rules for their application in music were first made by Carl Philipp Emanuel Bach, the most talented son of the great Johann Sebastian Bach, in his epoch making work "Versuch über die wahre Art das Clavier zu spielen" (Essay on the True Manner of Playing the Clavichord) (1753). He writes concerning grace notes: "They serve to connect the notes, they enliven them, and when necessary give them a special emphasis,... they help to elucidate the character of the music; whether it be sad, cheerful, or otherwise, they always contribute their share to the effect,..... an indifferent composition may be improved by their aid, while without them even the best melody may appear empty and meaningless." (English translation, in Grove's "Dictionary of Music and Musicians").

How strange this great praise of ornaments, sounds to modern ears; embellishments such as the Bebung (shaking), Schleifer (slide), Nachschlag (Aspiration), having entirely disappeared. The reason is to be sought in the difference of the keyboard instruments of that age and of ours, the tone of theirs being small, thin, short - lived, while the tone of our modern piano lasts, without pedal, two full $\frac{4}{4}$ measures in Andante, and even in Largo, and with pedal in Adagio Molto; also in the immense development of the organ and of the orchestra.

The ornaments which are of immediate interest and importance to us are the *Appoggiatura,* the *Acciaccatura,* the *Mordent,* the *Inverted Mordent* (in German the *Schneller,* or *Pralltriller),* the *Turn* and the *Trill.* All these, and many more, were, once upon a time, represented by certain mysterious signs; I say mysterious advisedly, because they were known to none except the initiated. Of all these many signs only the sign of the turn ∾ and of the arpeggiando ⌇ have survived. Haydn and Mozart used the Appoggiatura and Acciaccatura as well as the Mordents and Inverted Mordents very frequently. Beethoven very rarely uses the Appoggiatura; the Acciaccatura appears frequently, also the sign of Inverted Mordent is still retained. He uses very often the sign of the turn. With Beethoven the trill asserts itself beginning with the principal note. Chopin in only a few instances uses the Appoggiatura; the signs of the Inverted Mordent and of the Turn are retained. Likewise with Schumann. Liszt discards the Appoggiatura and also the sign of the

Inverted Mordent which, with him, is written out in full notes. The sign of the Turn is still retained, but does not occur often. Brahms usually writes out the ornaments in full.

Appoggiatura

This word comes from "appoggiare," which in Italian means "to lean on." It is one of the oldest of ornaments. It has no time-value of its own, but derives it from the *following note,* which thereby loses some of *its* value. The appoggiatura not only takes from the value of the note that follows it, but it also takes the accent from it. Therefore it *always* receives a *stronger accent* than that of the note with which it has been coupled.

Appoggiaturas have been divided into *long* and *short*. In both cases they appear written as *small notes*. Their written value is by no means an indication of the actual value which they take from the following, principal note. When meant as long appoggiaturas they usually appear written with half the value of the following note, but one also encounters them written with a shorter value. Their stem is seldom crossed, (♪ and not ♪̸) this last being, usually, the distinctive sign of the *acciaccatura*.

The *long appoggiatura* is the appoggiatura proper. It is always a *dissonant* note to the harmony, occurring on the upper or lower *auxiliary,* that is to say, a half step, or, at the most, a full step higher or lower than the note with which it is coupled, and always falls on the beats of the measure, or on accented parts of the beat. The appoggiatura, as already stated, takes the accent from the following written large note and, so to speak, resolves itself in it with a *legato* and *diminuendo* effect. If there were strict rules for knowing how much of the value of the principal note the appoggiatura takes to itself, there would be no trouble whatever. But, unfortunately, there are no strict rules. The value to be given to the appoggiatura depends on the value of the principal note, on the *measure* (whether double, triple or in 4/4 time) and on the *tempo*. On the whole the following rules may be considered as reliable, and followed implicitly.

If the value of the principal note can be divided into two equal parts the appoggiatura takes half the value of the principal note.

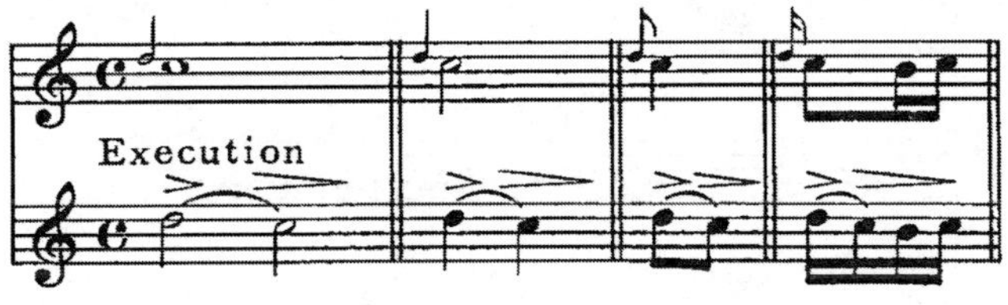

Andante from Sonata in D Minor
JOHANN SEBASTIAN BACH

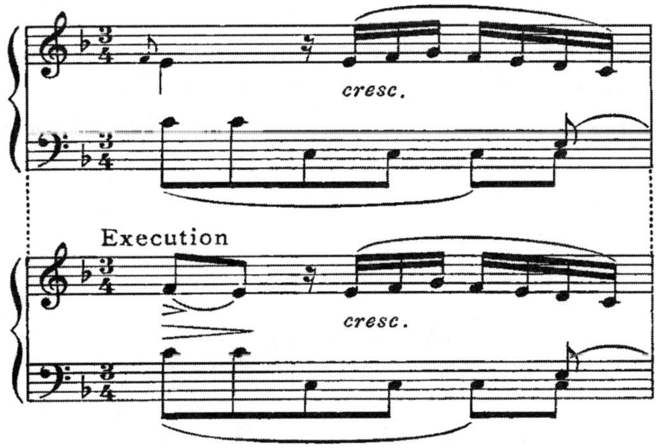

Aria with Variations (called Goldberg Var.)
JOHANN SEBASTIAN BACH

Sonata in A Major
WOLFGANG AMADEUS MOZART

When the principal note is dotted (𝅗𝅥. ♩. ♪. etc.) and cannot very well be divided into two equal parts, then the appoggiatura takes *two thirds* and leaves one third to the principal note. In other words the principal note retains only the value of the dot.

Toccata in G Minor
JOHANN SEBASTIAN BACH

If the principal note is tied to another note of the same degree and of equal or shorter value, then the appoggiatura takes the whole value of the principal note (first of tied notes), and the principal note retains the value of the second tied note.

Aria with Variations
JOHANN SEBASTIAN BACH

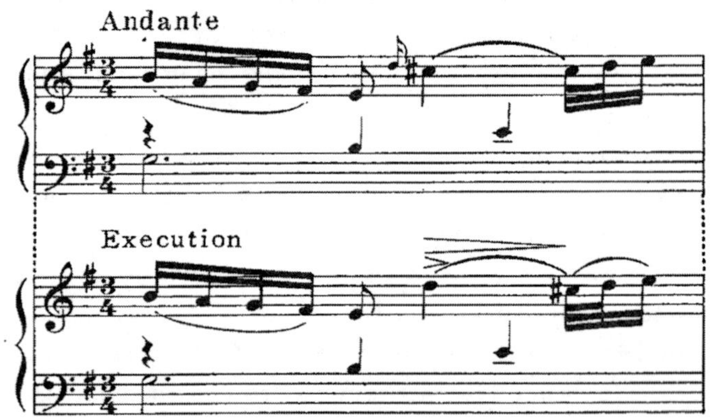

If the principal note, besides being tied to another note of equal degree and of equal or shorter value, is dotted, then the appoggiatura takes the whole value of the principal note *and of the dot*, and the principal note retains the value of the second tied note.

Air with 30 Variations
JOHANN SEBASTIAN BACH

In compound measures ($^6/_8$, $^9/_8$, $^{12}/_8$, etc.) the appoggiatura sometimes appears dotted:

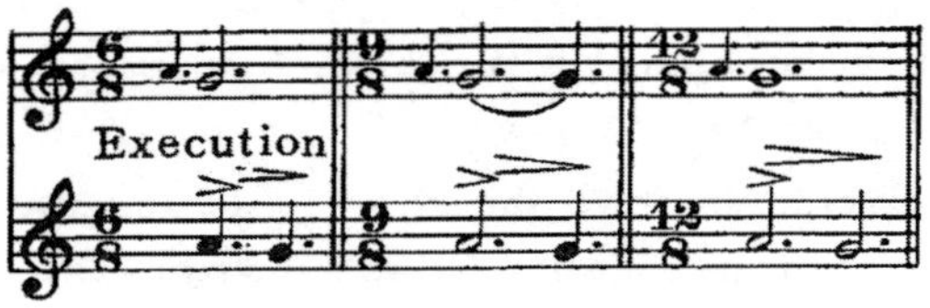

If the appoggiatura appears before a chord then *it becomes part of the chord,* and the note before which it is affixed is executed later, in accordance with the rules laid down:

Sonata in C Major
JOHANN SEBASTIAN BACH

Toccata in F♯ Minor
JOHANN SEBASTIAN BACH

When an appoggiatura appears before a trill, or an inverted mordent (Schneller, or Pralltriller), it is usually treated like a short appoggiatura (see further on). However, often the rules that govern the long appoggiatura are also applied in this case, as in the example given above.

In the case of an appoggiatura affixed to a note which is followed by a rest, the performer must keep in mind the clearly expressed intention of the composer to have the musical discourse cease with the appearance of the rest. This seems too evident to need dwelling upon. Yet, in the following example, from the C major Concerto of Beethoven, Franz Kullak, in the Steingräber edition, citing Carl Philipp Emanuel Bach's "Versuch über die wahre Art das Clavier zu spielen," advocates an execution which obliterates the rest entirely.

Concerto in C Major
LUDWIG van BEETHOVEN

Kullak says further that if Beethoven had wanted a shorter appoggiatura he would have written it out, as he has done in measure 37 of the *Largo*. I do not esteem this reason valid, nor should the authority of Carl Philipp Emanuel Bach be invoked in this case. Beethoven thought highly of Carl Philipp Emanuel Bach's book, it is true; but in his own compositions few appoggiaturas are found, and in nearly every case they seem to be the abbreviation of an appoggiatura fully written out a few measures before or afterwards. Thus too in this instance, as Kullak himself points out. Johann Sebastian Bach, also, has done this repeatedly. I give herewith an example that is to be considered as a parallel case to Beethoven's:

Sonata in D Minor
JOHANN SEBASTIAN BACH

In the two measures just before this passage, Bach writes out in full two appoggiaturas, both before a rest, and does so with due regard to the value and importance of that which is one of the most eloquent and effective means of expression in music: a rest. There is, therefore, the authority of J.S. Bach, the internal evidence in Beethoven's composition, as well as reasons of logic, for my contending that the correct execution of this passage is the following:

Short Appoggiatura

No rule is ever free from exceptions and therefore, it is no matter of wonder that there should be many cases where the rules laid down for a correct execution of the long appoggiatura cannot be adhered to. The reasons for departing from these rules are always substantial and well founded. The measure, the tempo, the rhythm, and a regard for euphony in polyphonic writing, these have necessitated a different treatment of the appoggiatura which, in every case, has had to be *shortened*, (never lengthened) thus giving birth to the short appoggiatura. Carl Philipp Emanuel Bach divided the appoggiatura into *variable* and *invariable* (short and long). Its nature and application in music are the same as the long appoggiatura, except that it only receives one third, or one fourth of the value of the principal note, at times even less. However, it preserves inviolate that which distinguishes the appoggiatura, whether long or short, the *accent*.

In the following example the appoggiatura, if considered as a long appoggiatura, would result in two consecutive sevenths:

Duet No. 4
JOHANN SEBASTIAN BACH

But the short appoggiatura conforms with the laws of counterpoint:

A long appoggiatura would result in two consecutive octaves in the following example. The application of a short appoggiatura is therefore necessary:

Sonata in C Major
JOHANN SEBASTIAN BACH

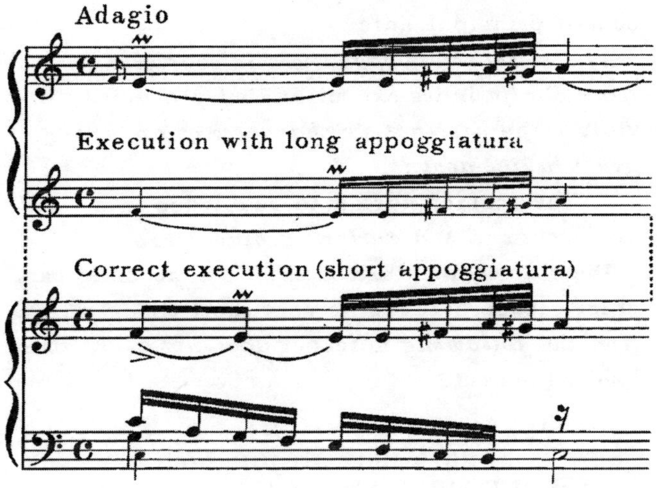

The Acciaccatura

The word *Acciaccatura* is Italian and is derived from the verb *acciaccare,* which means "to crush".

This grace-note has a very short time duration.

Our acquaintance with the appoggiatura (both long and short) has on the whole left us without disquiet, and the adherence to the rules which I have cited, and which are easy to remember, will result in a correct performance. Things, unfortunately, stand differently with the acciaccatura, and a deplorable divergence of opinion has existed among equally prominent musicians as to its correct execution. Already the fact that some composers have considered the acciaccatura an entirely different grace-note from the short appoggiatura, while others have not done so, adds to the confusion.

Leopold Mozart (father of the great Wolfgang Amadeus Mozart) *Hummel, Louis Köhler, Dr. Marx,* and others, all agree that in the case of the *short appoggiatura* (so they called the acciaccatura) the accent remains with the *principal* note.

As to the *length* of the short appoggiatura and whether it is to be derived from the note that follows or from the preceding note or rest there is considerable divergence of opinion among equally prominent authors, and, consequently, considerable confusion.

Eslava, the eminent Spanish theorist, gives as a rule that if the following note is of greater time value than the preceding note, then the short appoggiatura derives its time value from the following note, but if the preceding note is of greater time value then the short appoggiatura takes its *extremely short duration* from the *preceding note.* In case of equal values the tempo and the rhythm will be the deciding factors in determining where the appoggiatura belongs.

Le Carpentier calls the acciaccatura an *after-tone,* thereby implying that it derives its time value from the note or rest that *precedes* it. The same opinion is held by *Gaetano Nava* in his "Elements of Vocalization," who writes that "the imperceptible value of the acciaccatura is to be taken from the preceding beat." In the same sense many other prominent writers on music express themselves.

Dr. Calcott, in his "Grammar of Music," published in 1800, a work which, through its acknowledged sincerity has commanded much attention, makes mention of the "half beat" (in German "Zusammenschlag") and describes it as "a lower auxiliary tone, struck at the same time as the principal note and immediately quitted, very similar to the Italian acciaccatura." This takes for granted that the "Italian acciaccatura" is played, not before but with the principal note. Dr. Calcott adds that "when a small note *follows* a large one and *depends upon that* for its time, the name *after-note* (in German Nachschlag) will be used in this work to distinguish it from the appoggiatura."

Here I might also quote *Türk, Margburg, Stockhausen, Louis Köhler, Kalkbrenner,* and others.

The acciaccatura is considered by the greater part of modern German theorists as a sort of short appoggiatura which derives its time value, *always extremely short*, from the following note. Hans von Bülow confirms this but leaves the accent to the principal note.

This inflexible rule, notwithstanding the undoubted eminence of the musicians who have promulgated it, cannot always be applied. Its *unswerving application* would lead to distortions of the rhythm, of the measure. As a matter of fact it is not followed by the greatest virtuosos of our time, as anyone who has a keen musical ear and the faculty of quick perception and faithful retention can convince himself by listening to the performance of the classics by the acknowledged masters of the keyboard. *Dr. William Mason* backs up this statement when he says, in support of his contention that the short appoggiatura (acciaccatura) is to take its time value from the preceding note, that "the performance of the best pianists confirms this theory."

From this mass of statements is to be gathered that there is no divergence of opinion as regards the execution of the long appoggiatura, but that there is considerable confusion as to the execution of the acciaccatura, because some authors call it a short appoggiatura and some not; some want its time value derived from the *following* note, some from the *preceding* note, and Eslava, and with him some other prominent writers in music, want its time value determined by the greater or lesser value of the following or preceding note, this, by the way, being a sensible, logical rule. All agree that the acciaccatura (by some erroneously called short appoggiatura) does not, like the long appoggiatura, take to itself the accent, but leaves it to the *principal* note.

All this confusion may be avoided by the following classification:

1. The long appoggiatura is the appoggiatura proper and is designated "Appoggiatura." We have seen that it is always an upper or lower auxiliary, situated not farther than a full step from the principal note. It is always a dissonance. It always takes the accent and resolves itself, in a diminuendo, legato manner into the softer accented principal note.

2. The *short appoggiatura* is shorter, at times more abrupt in its execution, but preserves inviolate the *distinctive character of an appoggiatura, the accent.*

3. The acciaccatura is to be divided into *old acciaccatura* and *modern acciaccatura.*

The old acciaccatura occurs on an accented part of the measure, takes its very short time-value from the *following* note, but does *not* take the leading accent.

Sonata in C Major, No.5
WOLFGANG AMADEUS MOZART

Moment Musical, No.3
FRANZ SCHUBERT

The *modern acciaccatura* is executed *before* the note to which it is coupled. It is an *afternote* of the preceding note. It is a quick grace note which can be situated on any degree of the scale, not only (like the appoggiatura) on the upper or lower auxiliaries.

The question naturally rises: "When is an acciaccatura to be considered old or modern?" It is, indeed, not always easy to place it. But this may be said: in the older classics (Bach, Händel, Rameau, Couperin) and in the compositions of Haydn, Mozart and their contemporaries, we are generally dealing with the *old acciaccatura.* This applies, *at times only* to the works of Beethoven. Here we find often the *modern acciaccatura.*

This statement is in direct opposition to that of Hans von Bülow who repeatedly writes that "all grace-notes take their value from the following principal note". Eminent musician though he was, Hans von Bülow had a very hazy knowledge on the subject of ornaments, as is proved in numerous instances where double acciaccaturas are called by him appoggiaturas. He evidently did not know the *after-note,* nor the "tirata" nor "cadenza", for he never made mention of them.

Concerto in G Major
LUDWIG van BEETHOVEN

(See also the 3rd movement of the sonata in G major, Op. 31)

The *old acciaccatura* appears written in small notes, but the stem is not always crossed:

This is a source of much confusion and annoyance, for there is then nothing to show whether one is dealing with an appoggiatura or an acciaccatura, and only an intimate knowledge of the style of the classics, and of the subject of music ornaments will enable one to discern which is the correct execution.

The *modern acciaccatura* is also written in small notes, usually eighth or sixteenth notes, and the stem of the little note is *always crossed.*

The Double Acciaccatura

This embellishment is composed of *two notes* and originally consisted of the upper and the lower auxiliary, or *vice versa.*

It was formerly called "Anschlag" and under this designation it is described and commented upon by Carl Philipp Emanuel Bach in his "Versuch über die Wahre Art das Clavier zu spielen".

An example of this sort of grace-notes is found in the second movement of Beethoven's sonata Op. 81a.

The designation of double acciaccatura is now applied to an embellishment consisting of two notes situated on any degree of the scale. Its execution conforms in every way to the rules laid down for the single acciaccatura.

Sonata in D Major, No.15
WOLFGANG AMADEUS MOZART

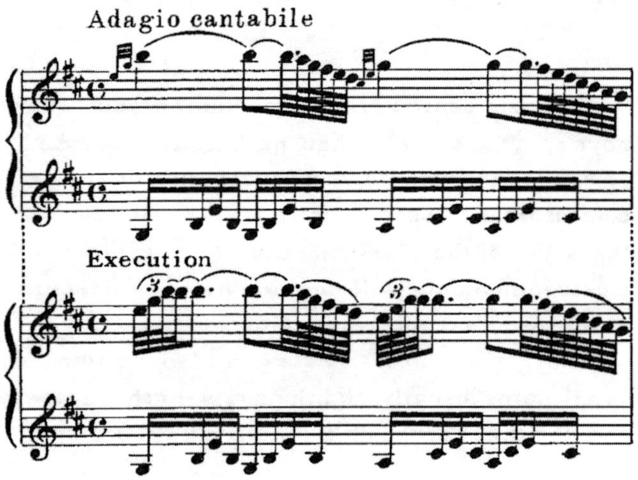

Mordent and Inverted Mordent

The mordent (in Italian *mordente*) consists of three notes: the principal note, the *lower* auxiliary note (situated a half-step, or a full step, lower) and again the principal note. The old sign for it was ⁓.

The inverted mordent uses the *upper* auxiliary note. That is the only difference between it and the mordent proper. The sign for it is ⁓.

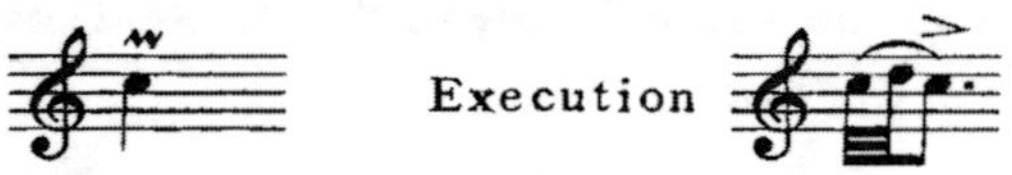

The first two quick notes must be played with abrupt shortness ("bitten off," as the Italian designation *mordente*, which is derived from *mordere* "to bite" fancifully suggests). These two first notes occur *always* on an accented part of the measure, and take their time-value from the *following* note. Regarding the accent, whether it should be given on the first note of the ornament or on the main note (the third note played) famous musicians have failed to agree upon. The advice of *Dannreuther* (Musical Ornamentation, page **169**) may be followed implicitly. He says that in quick tempo the accent should be on the first note of the ornament, in slow tempo on the main note. *Heinrich Germer* also supports this claim. When accenting the third (principal) note this is to be held until the time of the principal note is completed.

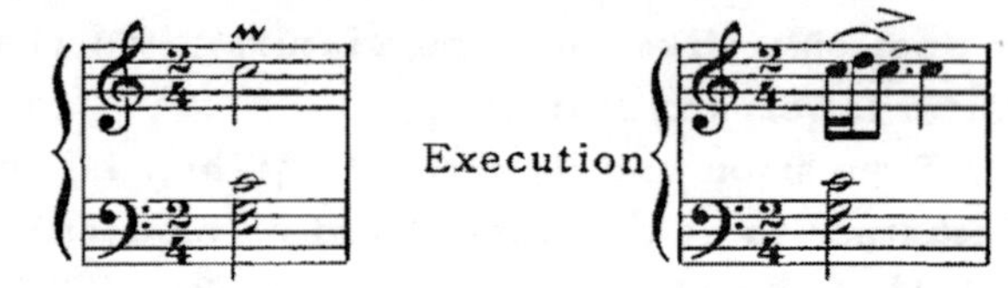

The speed with which the two first notes are to be played, as well as the location of the accent, depend on the *tempo* and on the duration of the principal note.

Two-Part Invention No. 1 in C major
JOHANN SEBASTIAN BACH

The inverted mordent is called in German *Schneller* and also *Pralltriller* (at times simply *Praller*). *Riemann*, in his "Musik Lexicon," and *Grove*, in his "Dictionary of Music and Musicians," make no distinction between the *Pralltriller* and the *Schneller*. Yet, there is a decided difference between both, as pointed out, long ago, by Dr. Calcott and by Carl Philipp Emanuel Bach.

The *Schneller* is the inverted mordent proper, as already explained and illustrated; it always has a delay on the principal note (third note played). The *Pralltriller* does *not* delay on the principal note; it transforms this principal note into a triplet:

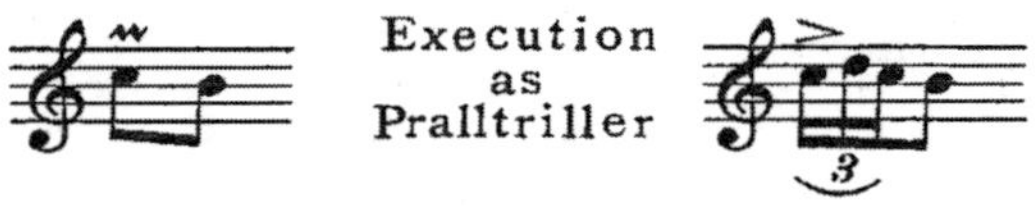

Carl Philip Emanuel Bach states that its usefulness is apparent only in passages descending by degrees:

As a matter of fact the descending degrees have less to do with this execution than the duration of the principal notes and the tempo which, if rapid, makes a triplet of the three notes and brings the *accent* on the first note played. Therefore the sign ⁓ is to be considered as a *Schneller* (inverted mordent, with delay on the principal note) in slow and in moderate tempo. But it becomes a *Pralltriller* (inverted mordent without delay on the principal note) whenever the tempo is so rapid that it becomes advisable to make a triplet of the three notes. This has a far-reaching influence on the execution of some well known compositions. In the sonata Op. 13 (Pathétique) by Beethoven, who has not had trouble with the following passage and those similar to it, trying to carry out the admonition, printed in many an edition, to begin the ornament on the beat and to delay on the principal note!

In his edition of this sonata Hans von Bülow writes: "Execution: 

"Beware of the facile and tasteless triplet in eighth-notes, to which even the anticipated passing shake would be preferable, though against the rules." In the tempo demanded by Beethoven it is almost impossible to execute the inverted mordents as *Schnellers* (with the delay on principal note demanded by von Bülow); a halting, awkward rhythm and an unavoidably jerky execution is the result. But if we view these inverted mordents as *Pralltrillers* (with no delay on the principal note) we follow the rules laid down by Carl Philipp Emanuel Bach and by Dr. Calcott and obtain an absolutely satisfying and at the same time brilliant and easy execution.

Thus also in the following examples:

Impromptu in A♭ Major, Op. 29
FREDERICK CHOPIN

Concerto in E Minor, for piano and orchestra
FREDERICK CHOPIN

Vivace (♩=104-112)

Concerto in C Major, for piano and orchestra
LUDWIG van BEETHOVEN
(1st movement)

Allegro con brio (♩=144-156)

When a note of short time-value is provided with a *Pralltriller* (𝆖) and is followed by a note situated a step or half-step lower, it is often impossible to play the usual three notes demanded by the *Pralltriller;* the result is, then, a turn formed by the *Pralltriller* and the next note. The following two examples are from Ludwig Klee's *"Die Ornamenthik"*:

The auxiliary note of both the mordent and the inverted mordent *must conform to the signature at the clef.* If the composer wishes that the auxiliary note should be flat, sharp or natural, the corresponding accidental must be written either above or below (as may be needed) of the sign 𝆗 or 𝆖. Examples:

When the mordent appears over a chord, then the first note of the ornament is played at the same time as the chord, and the remaining two notes are played afterwards:

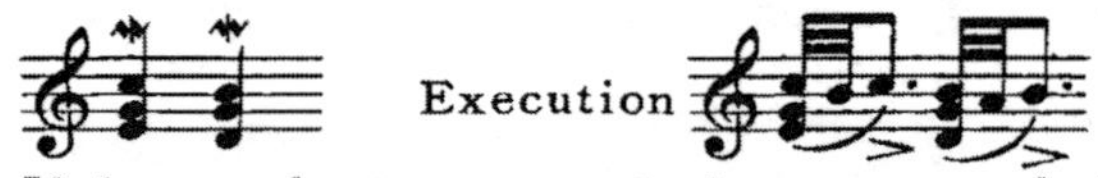

If the mordent appears before a note of the chord which is not the highest note of the chord, the execution conforms to the precepts already stated:

Little Prelude in C Major
JOHANN SEBASTIAN BACH

The *Pralltriller* is at times designated by the familiar sign of trill "*tr*" and appears thus very frequently in the works of Haydn, Mozart and even in those of Beethoven. There can, however, be no confusion between the *Pralltriller* and the trill proper, because the former appears written as "*tr*" only where a lively tempo makes a double shake, not to speak of a longer trill, impossible.

Sonata in D Major (Cotta edition No.4)
JOSEPH HAYDN

The inverted mordent appears frequently in modern music, but the old sign ⁓ is not used any more; the ornament is written out in full, in smaller type of notes. These little notes are usually played *before* the following note, with which they are coupled. They are to be considered, then, as *after-notes* of the preceding note or rest.

Danse Caprice Op. 28, No.3
EDVARD GRIEG

In all cases where one may find it difficult to decide upon the correct execution he should take into account the rhythm and the value of the notes *without* the ornament and conform the execution to them.

The Double Mordent

This grace note consists, as its name implies, in the repetition of the two little notes of the mordent or of the inverted mordent.

In every other way the execution is the same as that indicated in the Chapter of Mordents.

The Turn

In this chapter I do not purpose giving suggestions, advice and exercises for the acquisition of rapid brilliant turns and trills (this has been done in the chapters "Trills and Turns", Book III) but I do wish to indicate their correct execution as embellishments, that is to say, the correct execution of the signs which designate turns and trills, in accordance with the intentions of the composers and in accordance with the style (see the chapter "Style") in which their works should be played.

A turn is an embellishment consisting of a principal note with both its upper and lower auxiliaries. The execution is either: principal note, upper auxiliary, principal note, lower auxiliary and again principal note; or, the first principal note is left out.

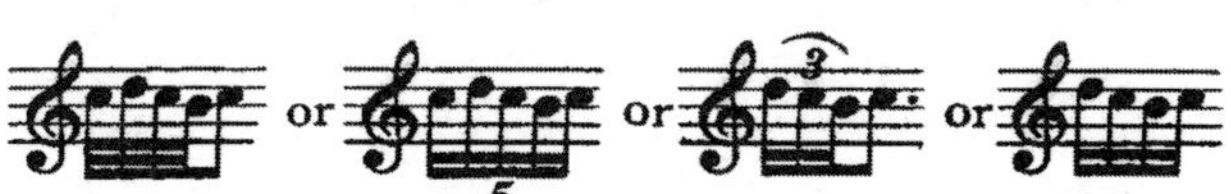

Turns are nearly always executed *legato* and they should be closely connected with the principal note to which they lead. One should remember that grace notes always lead to or encircle a principal note and that their mission is to beautify, to *embellish* this principal note, *without lessening its preponderant position.* As such the turn has ever taken a prominent place among grace notes, and indeed, conjointly with the trill, has survived all other forms. Therefore turns, like all graces, should be played as a general rule (there are exceptions) softer than the principal note to which they lead up with a crescendo. They may, at times, be played louder than the principal note, when they resolve into it with a diminuendo.

A turn, it will be seen, is composed of either five or of four notes. We shall presently know when the turn should begin on the principal and when on the auxiliary note.

The old-fashioned sign for the turn was and still is ∾. This means that the *first auxiliary* note is the *upper*.

When the turn was meant to have the *lower* auxiliary as *first* auxiliary note it was written thus: S.

If the composer wishes that the auxiliaries shoul be flat, sharp, or played natural, the corresponding signs are written above or below the sign of the turn.

The classical composers have often written the turn in small notes, instead of writing the sign ∾ or S. The rules for its execution are not, thereby, changed.

The correct execution of a turn depends, first, on the position of the sign of the turn in regard to the note; second, on the degree, on the staff, of the preceding note and of the following note; third, on the presence or absence of a dot after the note with which the turn is coupled (this does not apply to dotted notes which fill a measure, such as a dotted half-note in 3/4 time, or to dotted notes that fill a beat, such as dotted quarter-notes in 6/8, 9/8, 12/8, etc.); fourth, on the rhythm and the "meter" of the melodic design, on the structure of the phrase, and on the accompaniment.

When the sign of turn appears over a note situated between two adjacent notes (the notes just below and above it in the scale), it is best to begin the turn with the principal note. The turn is then composed of five notes.

Minuet in G Major

IGNACE JAN PADEREWSKI

When the sign of turn appears over a note preceded by a note of the same pitch, it may be executed in four different ways:

Beginning on the principal note;

Sonata in E♭ Major (Cotta edition No. 14)
JOSEPH HAYDN

Tying the principal note to the preceding note:

Sonata Op. 31, No. 2
LUDWIG van BEETHOVEN

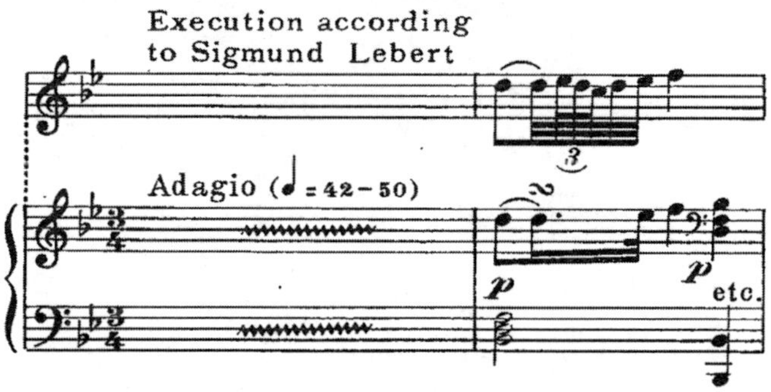

I believe that the following execution is to be preferred

Beginning on the upper auxiliary note:

Sonata in E♭ Major (Cotta edition No. 14)
JOSEPH HAYDN

Playing the turn *before* the principal note.

Rondo in C Major Op. 51, No. 1
LUDWIG van BEETHOVEN

When a turn is written out in small notes, instead of being indicated by the sign ∾, its execution, as has already been stated, is subject to the same rules:

Sonata in E♭ Major (Cotta edition No. 14)
JOSEPH HAYDN

In the following example it is evident that the turn cannot derive its time-value from the sixteenth note that precedes it; therefore it must take it from the following note:

Sonata in E♭ Major (Cotta edition No. 14)
JOSEPH HAYDN

Chains of turns

The *tempo* and the rhythm of a composition always play a preponderant role in the execution of grace-notes in general, and should be taken into consideration, whenever there is a doubt how to execute them. In the following examples the correct execution is indicated by a just observance of the rhythmic requirements.

Sonata in A♭ Major (Cotta edition No.16)
JOSEPH HAYDN

Execution according to Sigmund Lebert in his edition of the sonatas of Haydn:

but when the same passage re-appears later, a fourth higher, Lebert advocates an entirely different execution:

As a matter of fact, both executions are, in my opinion, incorrect. Adequate, correct executions are the following:

and

or

and

A somewhat similar case is found in the 1st movement of the sonata in C major, Op. 2, No.3 by Beethoven. Both the editions of Lebert and Faisst, and of d'Albert agree on the following execution, to which I also subscribe:

Sonata in C Minor, No.14 (Köchel No.457)
WOLFGANG AMADEUS MOZART

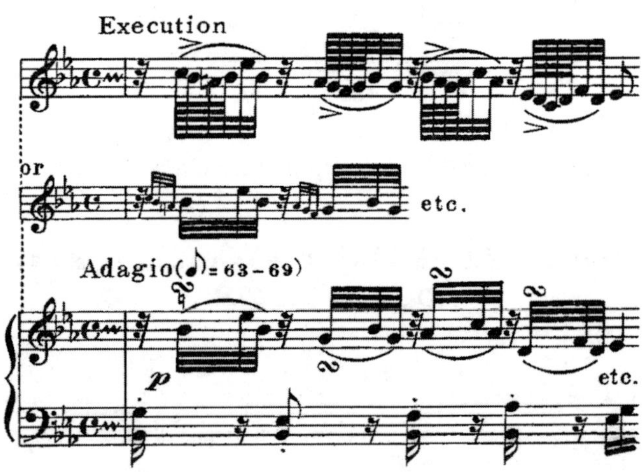

The *speed* of the turn depends also on the *tempo* in which it occurs and on the rhythmic life of the theme or of the whole phrase.

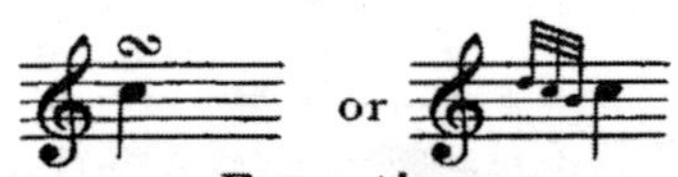

Execution

If the ∞ is placed *between* two notes which are *not* of the same degree, the turn begins with the upper auxiliary, consists of four notes, and there is *no delay* on the last principal note.

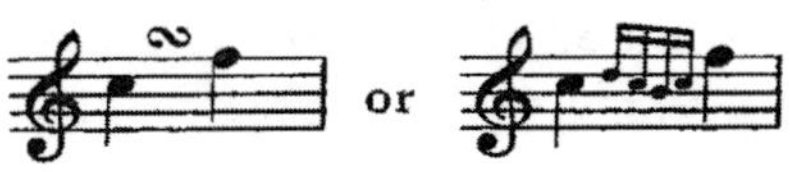

Execution

In slow tempo In moderate tempo In a rapid tempo

If the sign of the turn appears *between* two notes of *same degree or pitch*, the last principal note of the turn is not played, but is represented by the next common type note. In other words the turn *concludes* on the next common type note:

Execution

In slow tempo In moderate tempo

In a rapid tempo

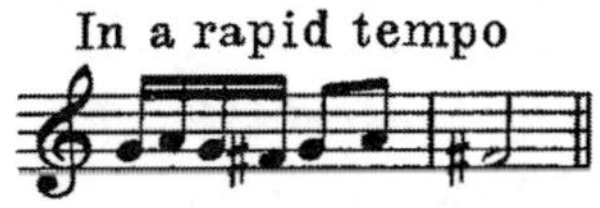

That there may be more than one correct way of interpreting the ancient symbols has already been stated. In his edition of the Cramer Etudes, Hans von Bülow gives *two* executions of the turn in the Etude in F minor, (No. 7, in the collection of fifty etudes). Hans von Bülow adds that he, however, prefers the latter, because "it more strictly maintains the rhythmical integrity of the melodic succession (syncopation of the second beat); neither can the dissonance of A♭ against the bass G (second half of second beat) be considered offensive."

Execution

Moderato con espressione

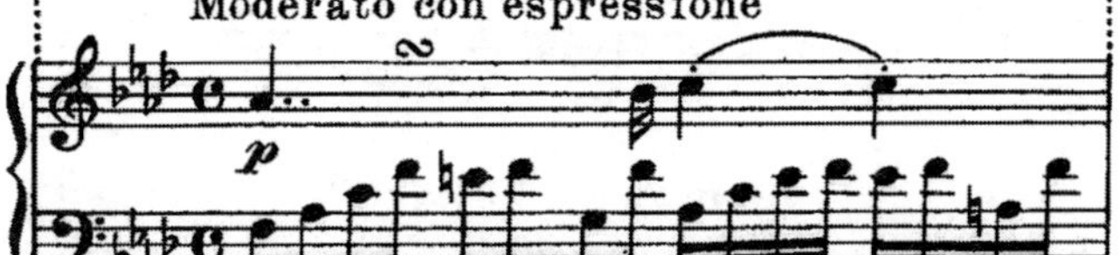

The following passage (the execution of the turn) has been interpreted variously by eminent musicians:

Sonata in C Minor, Op. 10, No. 1

LUDWIG van BEETHOVEN

Allegro molto e con brio (𝅗𝅥. = 69)

Execution according to Sigmund Lebert, in his edition of the sonatas of Beethoven:

Execution according to Ludwig Klee, in his "Die Ornamentik der Klavier-Musik":

(Carl Reinecke adopts this execution in his edition of the sonatas of Beethoven)

Two executions according to Eugène d'Albert, in his edition of the sonatas of Beethoven:

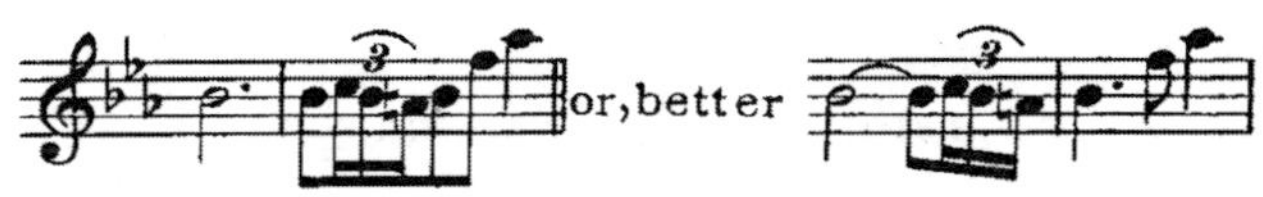

Possibly the following execution is preferable to any of the foregoing:

From what has been said so far it will be noticed that the attempt of a rhythmical division of the turn is given up in a rapid tempo. By rapid tempo is to be understood *Allegro vivace* or *Presto*.

When the sign of the turn appears after a dotted note, the second principal note of the turn (end of the turn) should be played at the exact moment where the dot takes effect, and be of equal (at times greater, but never lesser) time-value than the next common-type note. The execution is then actually the same as when the turn occurs between notes of same degree, because a dot written after a note is only a different way of writing out two tied notes of same pitch.

Sonata Op. 49, No. 1
LUDWIG van BEETHOVEN

Dr. Carl Reinecke confirms this when, in his "The Beethoven Sonatas" (Augener, London) he writes in regard to the Sonata Op. 14, No. 1: "The turn in the thirty eighth bar, induces me to quote the rule that when a turn is placed after a dotted note, the three notes of the turn must be played before the value of the dot, and that the principal note must be repeated at the place of the dot. Singular as this rule may appear to many, since the turn is placed *after* the dot, it is accounted for very easily if one realizes that it was formerly the custom, not as now to set the dot which lengthens the note by one-half immediately behind the note, but only at the place where it belongs in conformity with the division of the bar. Beethoven wrote:

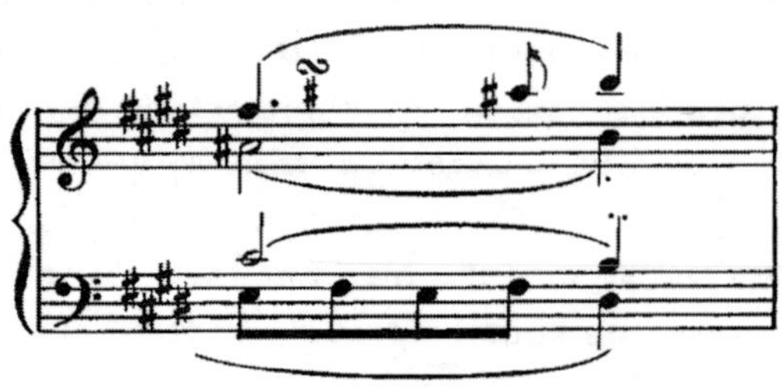

"and from this we perceive that the turn should be played before the third eighth note:

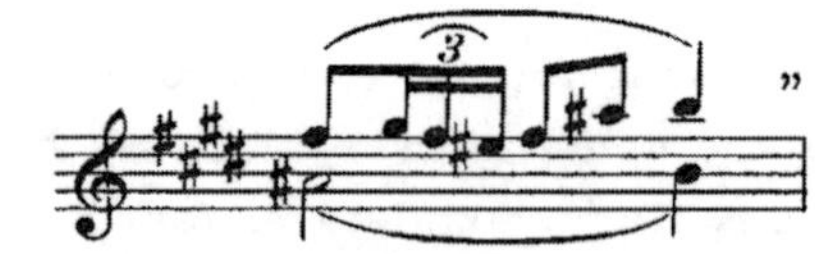

There are exceptions to this as to every other rule. In his edition of the sonatas of Beethoven, *Sigismund Lebert* says, in regard to the following passage in the first movement of the Sonata Op. 49 No. 1.

"Doubtless literally meant neither for  nor for  but "

If the turn appears after a *double dotted* note, then the last note of the turn (which is the principal tone) falls on the *first* of the two dots. This insures, *as a general rule*, greater rhythmical repose and firmness than if the last note of the turn falls on the second dot:

 Execution 

Sonata in C Minor, No. 14 (Köchel 457)
WOLFGANG AMADEUS MOZART

A turn preceded by an appoggiatura is to be executed during the value left to the principal note:

Sonata in A♭ Major (Cotta edition No.16)
JOSEPH HAYDN

When the sign of the turn appears over a double-note (third or sixth), it affects only the upper note.

Sonata in C♯ Minor (Cotta edition No.8)
JOSEPH HAYDN

The composer who wants a turn in double-notes should write it out, as has been done by Beethoven in the first movement of his Concerto in E flat major, for piano and orchestra.

The sign of the inverted turn ∾ is never found in the compositions of Haydn, Mozart and Beethoven. They always wrote it out in small-type notes. Its execution conforms in every way to the rules laid down for the turn proper. The inverted turn is found quite frequently in the compositions of the afore-mentioned masters of classical music. Its effect and brilliancy is instanced with peculiar force in the Overture of "Der Freischütz," by C. M. von Weber.

Sonata in E♭ Major, Op.7
LUDWIG van BEETHOVEN

Some readers may think that too much space has been given in this work to the study of such an apparently innocuous embellishment as the turn. Let them, however, compare the turn with the other embellishments which we possess in music and they will acknowledge that with the exception of the trill it leads them all. Strictly speaking, it is no embellishment at all, but an idiomatic expression of the cantilena. This is shown in numerous instances, among others in the aforementioned first movement of the concerto in E flat major, by Beethoven; in the first movement of the B♭ major sonata (570, Köchel) by Mozart; in the "Eusebius" of the *Carnaval*, by Schumann, and more so in the third movement (*Adagio ma non troppo, con affetto*) of Beethoven's sonata,

Op. 101. This might indeed be termed the apotheosis of the turn, for it assumes there a tenderness of expression, a loftiness of ideals and a thematic significance hardly paralleled elsewhere.

How highly Beethoven valued the turn as a means of expression is shown by the fact that in his thirty two sonatas for piano he used it no less than four hundred times! Haydn used the turn still more lavishly. In twenty of his sonatas for piano it appears four hundred nine times. This compilation, so far as I know, has not been made before; yet, who will deny its significance?

The Trill
(Also called Shake)

Two origins have been given to the trill.

According to Carl Philipp Emanuel Bach, Margburg and Türk, the trill, or shake, is derived from the *appoggiatura* and consists of an uninterrupted series of appoggiaturas and their resolutions. Therefore, according to them, the trill must begin on the upper or side note; and on this side note, the initial accent falls.

Carl Philipp Emanuel Bach seemingly endorsed this view when he wrote (in 1753) that "until now the trill was used only after an appoggiatura or when repeating the preceding note; in the first case one called it the *connected trill*. Nowadays it appears at the beginning of passages in skips, in succession of trills, in cadences, also after long holds, at the beginning of periods without preceding appoggiatura and also after these. Consequently, this ornament is used now with more freedom than formerly." He gives the following example:

This view seems to have been supported by Johann Sebastian Bach, who considered the trill as a dissonance, which had to begin on the *side-note* and which usually required the "after beat" or "after-turn" (See, further on, examples and exceptions).

Against this theory may be upheld the following: the trill owes its origin to the gradually accellerated motion of *one tone:* This was soon after developed into the gradually accellerated alternation of a tone and its side-note. In his "Singing School" (published in 1601) *Giulio Caccini* describes the *trillo* as taught by him to his pupils, stating that it consists of the rapid repetition of a single note.

Caccini makes also mention of another ornament which he calls *Gruppo;* it will be seen that it bears close resemblance to our modern trill:

G. Caccini (1550 - 1618)

In his "Lexicon der Tonkunst", by *Schilling*, (7 volumes, 1835-40), Conforti (or Consorti) is given as the name of a singer in Rome, in 1591, who first used the modern trill, consisting of two tones on conjoint degrees, in rapid alternation. Therefore, so far as known, it was a singer who first employed the trill, an ornament which, in its virtuoso sense, is best executed on instruments.

Originally the trill (see Dannreuther's "Musical Ornamentation") was divided into the *Battement:-*

and in the *Ribattuta* (in German *Zurückschlag*):-

(See, further on, the execution, according to Gevaert and to Wouters, of the trills in the G minor Prelude, Book I, in the Well Tempered Clavichord of Bach).

The modern sign for the trill is *tr* which is

placed always *over* the note that should be trilled. If the trill is of long duration the two letters *tr* are followed by an undulating line which terminates when the trill stops: ~~~~~~

In the older classics (before Haydn and Mozart) the trill was indicated by either *tr* or by ~~~; or by ~ (which last sign is really the sign for the inverted mordent); or (more rarely so) by + and ⌒⌒⌒⌒. All these signs appeared generally above but at times also under the note.

Execution of the Trill

A trill is executed with the principal note (the note which is written on the staff, and over which appears the sign *tr*.) and with the side-note. This side-note is *always* the note situated a half or a full step (never more than a full step) immediately above the principal note; it is *never* the note immediately below it.

The side-note of the trill is to be played according to its designation in the signature at the clef. For example, in the following trill:

the D, which is the side-note, is to be played flat because it appears so in the signature at the clef. In the following trills:

 and 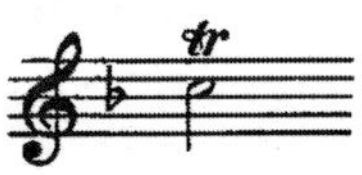

the D is played "natural" because it is "natural" in the signature.

If a sign of accidental appears over the sign *tr*. it affects the side-note accordingly. For example:

 Execution 

 Execution 

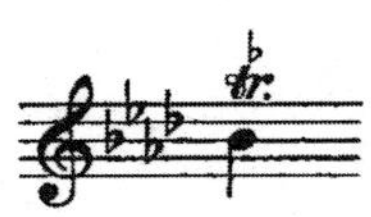 Execution 

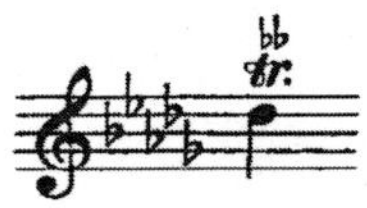 Execution 

 Execution 

 Execution 

In some cases, however, eminent composers have not written the required accidental over *tr*. because the preceding note being of the same degree as the side-note, had the necessary accidental, or because a modulation made it seem to them unnecessary to add accidentals over the *tr*.

Symphonic Etudes
(Variation VII)
ROBERT SCHUMANN

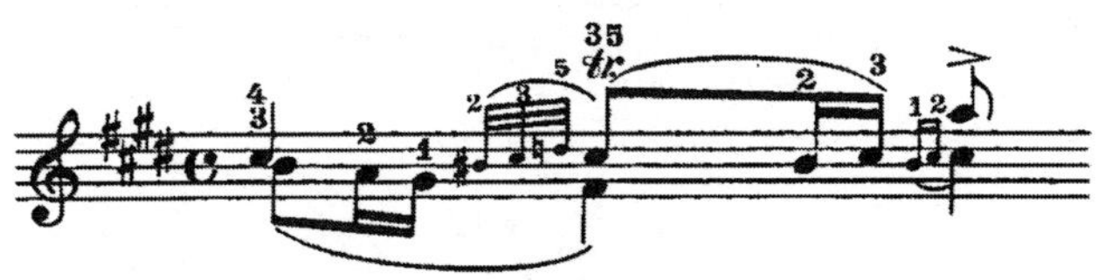

Execution

Ballade in A♭ Major
FREDERICK CHOPIN

Execution

Such a practice, notwithstanding the greatness

of the two composers cited, is not to be commended.

The sign *tr.* written over a double-note (third, fourth, sixth or octave) affects only the upper note. When written under the lower note it affects the lower note only.

Prelude in F Major, (Book I)
of the Well Tempered Clavichord
JOHANN SEBASTIAN BACH

Allegretto

etc.

If the composer wants both notes to be trilled the sign *tr.* must be affixed to both upper and lower note.

Barcarolle
FREDERICK CHOPIN

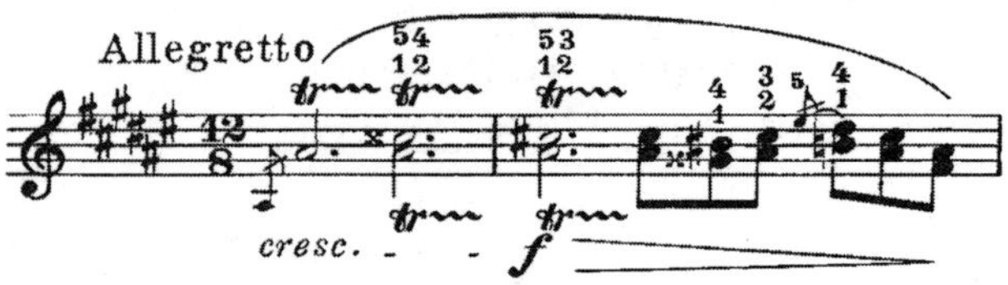

How to begin the Trill

A trill begins on either the principal or on the side-note, according to circumstances, to the period of time in which the composition was written and especially according to the style of, as well as to the views held by, the composer in regard to the execution of trills.

Nowadays, in accordance with the views held already by Beethoven, a trill is considered to begin on the principal note.

If the trill is meant to begin with the side-note (or with a note lower than the principal note) this is indicated by a grace-note written before the principal note.

Sonata Op. 57
LUDWIG van BEETHOVEN

etc.

etc.

Sonata Op. 10, No. 2
LUDWIG van BEETHOVEN

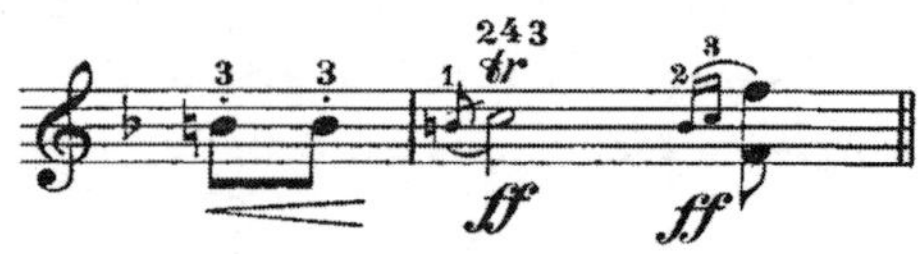

etc.

Unless otherwise indicated a trill ends nowadays usually with what is designated as the "after-beat" or "after-turn". This is composed of the principal note, then the note situated half a step below it and again by the principal note.

(See, further on, examples and exceptions.)

A trill should be executed as rapidly as consistent with distinctness and without rhythmical division of the notes.

In a slow tempo trills of a certain length are best begun by playing slowly the first two or three notes and then quickly increasing the speed. In a rapid tempo the same procedure may be employed if the trill is very long, but in shorter trills it is usually best to emphasize the melodic value of the trilled note by a very slight delay, or by a moderate accent, on the first note of the trill, followed immediately by rapid trilling.

Prelude in G Minor, (Book I)
of the Well Tempered Clavichord
JOHANN SEBASTIAN BACH

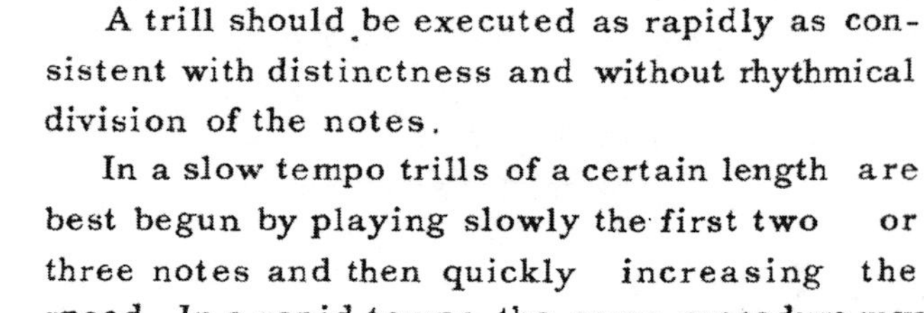

Execution according to the *Ribattuta* sponsored by Francois Auguste Gevaert and published in the Wouters edition of the Well Tempered Clavichord.

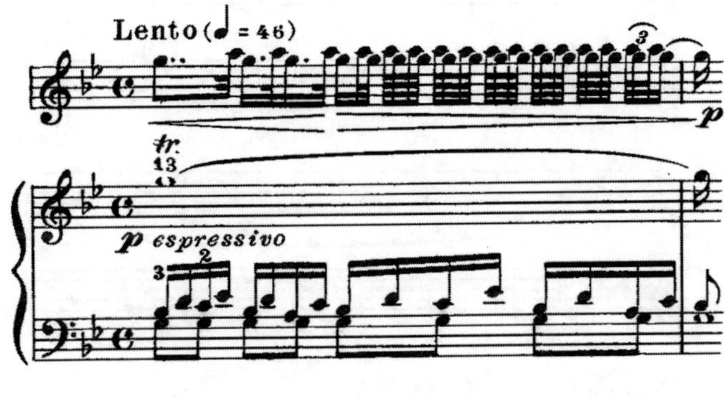

A trill is to be played with measured notes, that is to say, with a given number of 8th, 16th, 32d or 64th notes, or triplets, when the bass or the melodic notes connected with the trill make this mode of execution necessary.

Three Part Invention in C Minor

(Busoni edition)

JOHANN SEBASTIAN BACH

(See also the chapter "Trills", Book III)

Before the time of Beethoven

In the time of the early clavichordists, later in the time of Bach and Händel, and still later in the time of Haydn and Mozart, trills were generally begun with the *side-note*. When the composer wanted the trill to begin differently he wrote a short appogiatura or an acciaccatura before the trilled note, to indicate how the trill should begin.

Yet, the instances were not few where it was deemed imperative to begin with the *principal* note.

According to Grove's "Dictionary of Music and Musicians" the trill was made to begin on the principal note in the following cases. (These rules hold good to this day):

The Trill begins on the Principal Note

1. At the commencement of a phrase.

Fugue XIII, in F♯ Major, Book II
of the Well Tempered Clavichord

JOHANN SEBASTIAN BACH

Allegro

See also Prelude in G minor, Book I, already cited).

2. After a rest.

Sonata in E♭ Major
WOLFGANG AMADEUS MOZART

Allegro

3. After a skip.

Fugue, in the Suite in E Minor
GEORG HÄNDEL

Maestoso

Art of Fugue (No. 8)
JOHANN SEBASTIAN BACH

4. When the preceding note is of the same pitch and is marked staccato. When not marked staccato, the trill begins on the side-note. (See further on).

Sonata in C Minor
WOLFGANG AMADEUS MOZART

Molto allegro

Execution 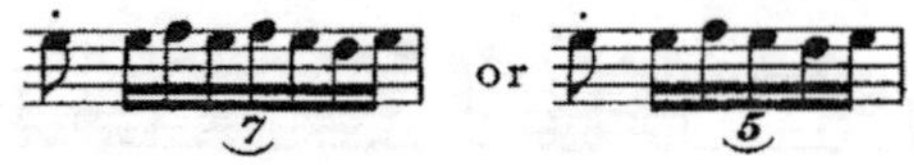

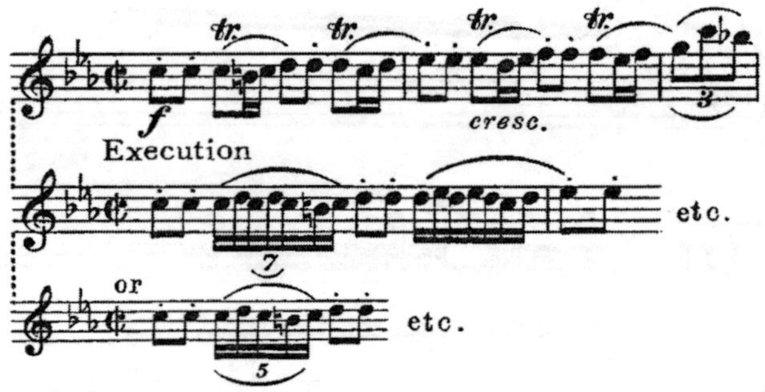

5. After a note situated one degree above or below. This preserves the melodic sequence. A real trill, which requires *at least* four notes, is possible then only in a slow or moderate tempo. But in a rapid tempo the trill becomes a *Pralltriller* (see "Inverted Mordent").

Sonata in C♯ Minor (Cotta edition No. 8)
JOSEPH HAYDN

Menuetto

Moderato (♩ = 126)

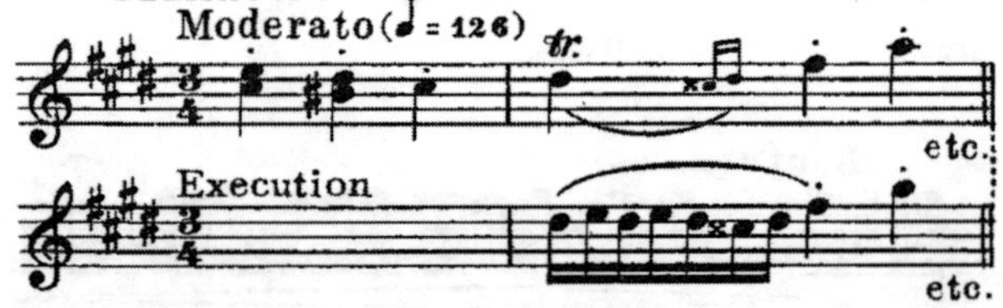

Sonata in D Major (Cotta edition No. 13)
JOSEPH HAYDN

Allegro assai (♩ = 144–148)

Since the Time of Beethoven

Beethoven was the first great composer to demand that instead of being an exception, the beginning of the trill on the principal note should be the rule. This is the manner in which the trills that abound in his compositions should be executed. Whenever he wanted the trill to begin differently he was careful to preface it with a grace-note. Examples have already been cited. Composers, nowadays, proceed in the same manner.

We have seen that the older classics considered the beginning of the trill on the principal note an exception and gave rules to indicate it.

From a modern standpoint the reverse takes place. Following are the cases where, from the modern point of view, a beginning on the side-note is imperative, or, at least, desirable:

The Trill begins on the Side-Note

1. When the preceding note, whether a normal note or a grace-note, is of the same pitch and of short time-value.

Chromatic Fantasy and Fugue
(Wouters Edition)
JOHANN SEBASTIAN BACH

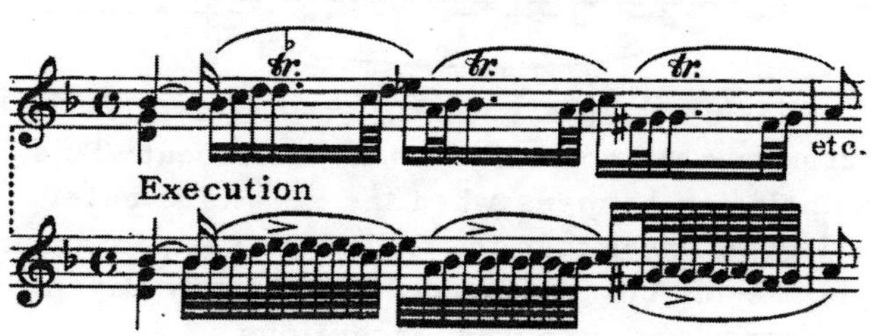

Barcarolle
FREDERICK CHOPIN

(See also examples, given further back, of the Sonata Op. 57, by Beethoven)

2. When the preceding note is situated a degree higher than the trilled note and is connected with it by a slur. The trill begins then with the side-note tied to the preceding note. Such was the acknowledged rule for compositions prior to the time of Beethoven; it was called the tied trill (in German, *gebundene Triller*).

Concerto in C Major
by HERZOG JOHANN ERNST
von Sachsen-Weimar
arranged for the Clavier by J.S. Bach

3. When preceded by an appoggiatura, the appoggiatura then begins the trill. Such cases are extremely rare in modern music where appoggiaturas are written out in normal notes.

Sonata Op.57
LUDWIG van BEETHOVEN

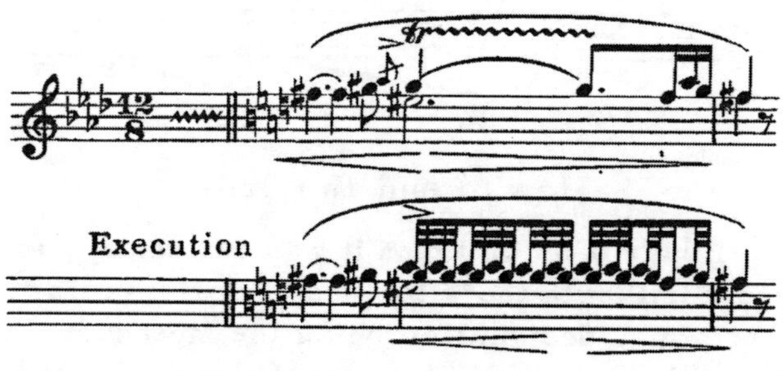

In the piano compositions of Bach, Händel and their contemporaries, trills are often found coupled to signs that indicate more preparatory notes than the simple side-note. They are described further on under the title "Obsolete Signs". In modern music such elaborate beginnings of a trill are found also, but the composer takes care to write these initial notes as grace notes. This commendable practice was indulged in by Haydn and Mozart.

Sonata in C Major, No.5
WOLFGANG AMADEUS MOZART

Sonata in B♭ Minor
FREDERICK CHOPIN

How to end the Trill

Already in olden times it was customary to end a trill with the "after-beat" or "after-turn", the former designation being the most suitable and corresponding to the German word *Nachschlag*. This after-beat, already described, is often expressly indicated by the composer. A single grace-note, situated a half-step below the principal note, is sufficient to indicate the required after-beat if the note that follows the trilled note is of the same pitch.

But if the note that follows the trilled note is situated one or more degrees higher or lower, the after-beat is indicated by two grace-notes, or by normal notes. Such was the usual practice of Haydn, Mozart, Beethoven and Schubert.

Sonata Op. 31, No.1
LUDWIG van BEETHOVEN

Sonata Op.143
FRANZ SCHUBERT

Sonata Op.147
FRANZ SCHUBERT

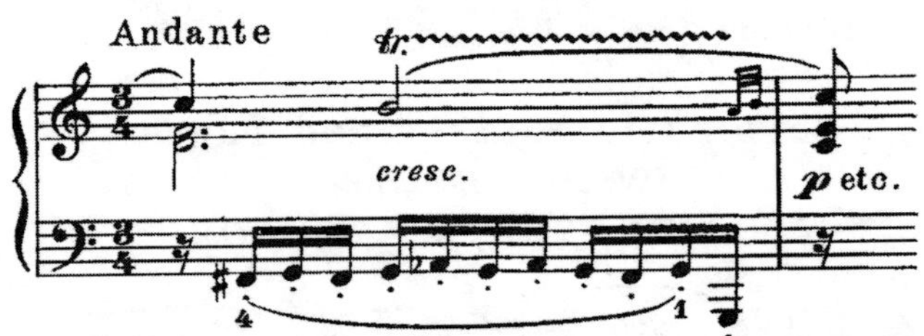

Examples are not wanting where a trill melts into the next note without an after-beat. This sometimes happens when the note is situated a degree lower than the trilled note (see example already cited: Sonata in D major, by Haydn).

There are, of course, exceptions.

Sonata in E♭ Major, Op.31, No.3
LUDWIG van BEETHOVEN

At times the trill ends abruptly on the principal note. Such is, usually, the case when the trill is followed by a rest and no "after-note" is written out.

Sonata Op.101
LUDWIG van BEETHOVEN

If the trilled note is tied to the following note, both being of the same pitch, it was formerly customary to end the trill on the principal note and tie it to the following note (see example cited of the Prelude in G minor, Book I, by Bach).

There are cases, though, where it is necessary, for harmonic reasons, to end in a different way, by adding, at the end of the trill, the side-note.

Sonata in B♭ Major
WOLFGANG AMADEUS MOZART

If the sign of the trill is over a dotted note the trill is often made to stop on the principal note when the dot takes effect. This is the same rule that has been given in the execution of turns.

Suite 10, Allemande
GEORG HANDEL

Exceptions may be cited here too. In many cases it is best to trill continuously until the after-beat. The dot is then considered as a continuation (tied note) of the principal note.

Sonata in C Major, No.3
WOLFGANG AMADEUS MOZART

Chains of Trills

When the chain of trills occurs in a descending direction none of the trills ends with the "after-beat" (See example: Nocturne by Chopin, Book III, pages 216 to 218).

When the chain of trills occurs in ascending direction, it is often the last trill only that receives an after-beat.

Concerto in E♭ Major
LUDWIG van BEETHOVEN

See also the much longer "chain of trills" in the same movement of the concerto, at the end of which Beethoven wrote the after-beat.

In some cases, though, every trill has the "after-beat".

Ballade in A♭ Major
FREDERICK CHOPIN

Sometimes more elaborate endings of a trill are written out in full, or as grace notes (see examples cited of the Sonata Op. 57, by Beethoven).

The Sign of Arpeggio

In modern music the sign ⦚ placed before a chord means that it is to be arpeggiated from bottom upward:

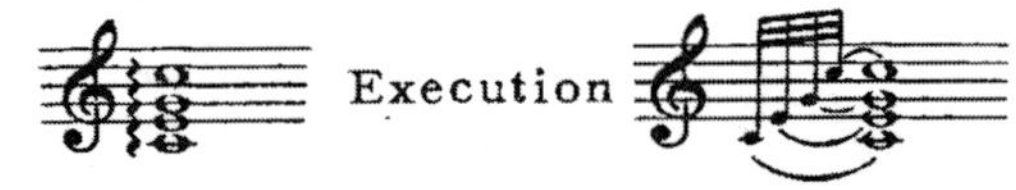

It is never arpeggiated from the upper note downward, unless the composer writes this out expressly, in small-type notes:

Symphonic Etudes
(Variation No. 8)
ROBERT SCHUMANN

Many theorists have adopted the rule that when the sign ⦚, standing before two chords which have to be played, at the same time, by both hands, is unbroken, the execution becomes an uninterrupted arpeggio, from the lowest note in the bass to the highest in the treble.

Sonata in D Minor, Op.31, No.2
LUDWIG van BEETHOVEN

"The arpeggio should be executed quietly and ought not to shorten the duration of the highest note, as half-note, in proportion to the following quarter-notes, play thus:"
(Foot-note by Sigmund Lebert in his edition of the Beethoven Sonatas)

Execution according to Hans von Bülow

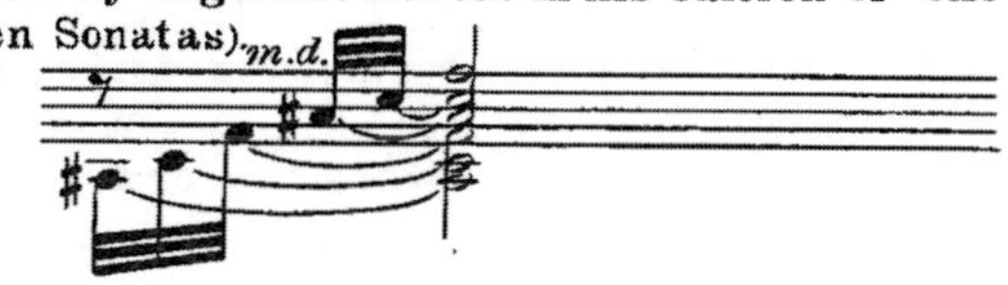

But if the sign is not continuous from the lowest note to the highest, that is to say, if there is a short alloted to each chord the performer plays the two arpeggios simultaneously, striking together the first note in each chord and ending the last notes together.

Sonata Op. 57 (Appassionata)
LUDWIG van BEETHOVEN

In most cases, especially if there are more notes in one chord than in the other, it will be found advantageous and of better effect to execute the arpeggiated chords uninterruptedly, from the lowest note to the highest.

In Bach's time the direction of the arpeggios was sometimes indicated by these signs:

meant to arpeggiate from the bottom upward.

or meant to arpeggiate from the highest note downward.

At that time, the sign of arpeggio was often meant to extend far beyond the written notes. It is interesting, in this case, to observe the simplicity of annotation and the richness of the result in the execution.

In his Chromatic Fantasy and Fugue Bach wrote:

The author of this work has employed to indicate the ascending direction of the arpeggio, and for the descending direction (see the chapter "Arpeggios" Book III, page 31 and following).

The Tremolo

In the 16th century the tremolo was for every instrument, the rapid repetition of *one tone*. It is still considered as such in the case of string instruments.

On the piano we now look on it as a more or less rapid (usually as rapid as possible) alternation of two, three, four or even five tones:

Modern composers are usually careful to write out in full the notes to be played. Still, the sign of the tremolo  is encountered quite frequently.

Formerly the most accepted sign for the tremolo was the following:

 Execution 

If 64th notes were wanted then the stem of the note or chord was crossed by *four* little lines. This manner of indicating the tremolo is found often in the compositions of Bach.

The Cadenza

(In Italian *cadenza* and also *tirata*)

This embellishment comprises an unrestricted number of notes. They always appear written in small-type notes, and take their time-value in some cases from the preceding note or rest.

Nocturne in A♭ Major, Op.32, No.2
FREDERICK CHOPIN

In other cases the time-value is taken from the following note. Whenever necessary the tempo may be slightly ritarded, in order to enable a smooth execution.

Ballade in A♭ Major
FREDERICK CHOPIN

These little grace-notes should always be played softer than the principal tones; they should usually be played legato, with a lighter touch, and *in one way or another* they must always *lead up* to and *embellish* the *next principal tone*. This applies to every *ornament;* it should help to beautify, not to deface. And it should never be so crudely or rudely prominent as to overshadow or hide entirely the fundamental melodic design on which it is embroidered. In order to lead well unto the next principal tone a crescendo, or a diminuendo, or a ritard will often be found advantageous.

After - Notes

Mention has already been made of them in the division of this chapter entitled "Appoggiatura".

Although known and described by the old theorists, mentioned and explained in Riemann's "Musik Lexikon", in Grove's "Dictionary of Music and Musicians", and more especially, in all the leading treatises on musical ornamentation, employed by Bach and by Händel, the after-notes are, strange to say, unknown to many an otherwise well-schooled and competent modern musician. Even such an eminent artist as Hans von Bülow seems to have ignored their existence, for in a footnote to the sonata Op. 57 (Appassionata), in his edition of the sonatas of Beethoven, he writes: "As in the case of all embellishments, without exception, the first three notes must fall precisely on the count to which they belong." That "without exception", as well as similar observations in other foot-notes, proves that Hans von Bülow was not conversant with a form of musical ornamentation that had won the approval of the older classicists and which has survived to this day.

Briefly described, the after-note (it may be represented by a single note or by many) is a grace note that depends for its time-value *not* on the following note but on the preceding note with which, in olden times, it generally appears connected by a slur.

(From "Embellishments of Music", by Louis Arthur Russell)

If the after-note consists of a single note, it is equal to a *modern* acciaccatura (see above, example of Beethoven's Concerto for piano, in G major). If, as in the example just given this ornament consists of two notes, it is then usually either a "slide" or an inverted mordent, (see above, example of Grieg's "Dance Caprice)."

An interesting and instructive example of three grace-notes is found in the Rondo, "Alla Turca", of the sonata in A major, by Mozart. So far as I know all editions of this celebrated composition make it a point to write a foot-note in which the reader is urged to play the grace-notes "on the beat", that is to say, to strike the first of the three grace-notes with the octave in the right hand.

If the editors who wrote that foot-note had listened more carefully to their own playing, or to the playing of others, they would, at once, have detected that they were not playing what Mozart wrote. For, instead of playing, as principal notes, the *four* A's written by Mozart, they played only *three*.

Such is, indeed, one of the two unavoidable modes of execution, if the pianist tries to play the first of the three grace-notes "on the beat". The other execution results from trying to preserve the four A's written by Mozart; the outcome is a rhythm changed to such an extent as to make a burlesque of a singularly captivating and effective passage:

But if these grace-notes are considered as *after-notes* to be played immediately *after* the preceding principal note and *before* the following principal note - the whole difficulty vanishes at once; the rhythm becomes natural and incisive, the accents forceful and the execution easy.

For the same reason of rhythmic precision and firmness and of metrical accentuation, I recommend, in contradistinction to the advice offered in all the afore-mentioned editions, to consider as after-notes the double acciaccaturas in the first period of the Rondo "Alla Turca":

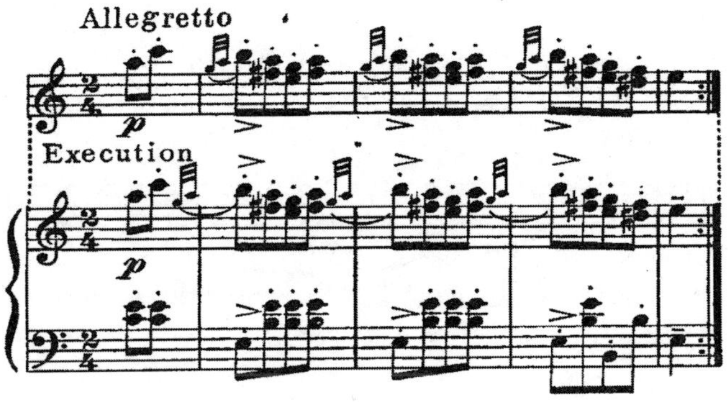

Obsolete Signs

Their description and study belongs more properly to the special treatises written on musical ornamentation. If a few are mentioned, briefly, in this chapter it is only because these obsolete signs are reproduced, without comment or explanation, in many a modern edition of the piano compositions of Bach, Händel and their contemporaries. A cultured musician should know their correct execution, without the aid of an explanatory edition. A good example is offered by the three Part Invention No. 5 in E flat major, of Bach. In many an otherwise fine edition the obsolete signs are reproduced without comment or explanation. Compare these editions with the written-out execution in the editions of Ferruccio Busoni (Breitkopf & Haertel) and of William Mason (G. Schirmer, New York).

The sign ∽∿ means that the trill is to begin with the lower, adjacent note; this gives the impression of beginning the trill with an inverted turn.

If the hook, at the beginning, goes up: ∽∿, then the trill starts as follows: upper side-note, principal note, lower side-note followed by the trill proper, giving the impression of beginning with a turn. See, at the end of this chapter, the table of signs written by Bach.

In his "Die Ornamenthik in der Klavier Musik," Ludwig Klee gives the following execution of the obsolete signs in the Two Part Invention No. 9, by Bach:

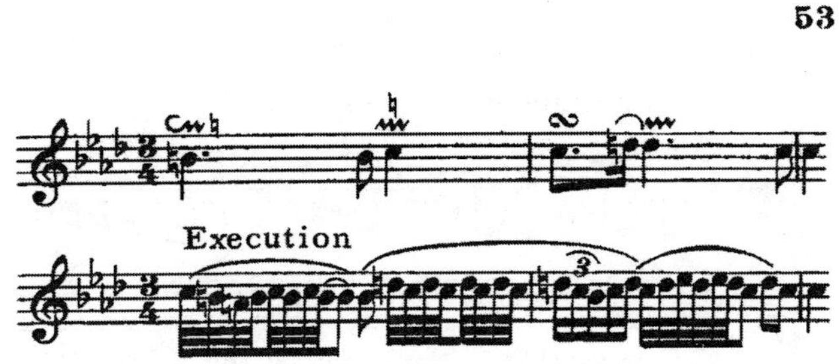

Compare the above with the following simplified execution given by Busoni in his edition of the same Invention. It is a compromise between an execution that was in vogue in the days of the clavichord and clavicembalo (or harpsichord) and that which corresponds to modern spirit. This attitude is reflected in the "Editor's Preface" of the Augener edition of the Händel Suites: "The numerous ornaments which were necessary for the instruments in use in Händel's days are given above the notes, but as our modern instruments do not require them, they are left unnoticed".

Sometimes the sign is crossed by a small vertical line: ∽∿| or ∽∿| or ∿|. This means that the trill ends with the after-beat. Such is also the meaning of the double sign ∾ over ∿ or ∿ ∾. The difficulty of the execution of some of these obsolete signs is often entirely out of proportion to the simplicity of the piece in which they appear. Thus in the Little Prelude in C major (1st Prelude for beginners) by Bach, appears the following:

Easier is the execution sponsored by Kühner, in the Litolff edition; by Dr. Mason in the Schirmer edition; and by Buonamici, also in the Schirmer edition:

The Slide or Slur

(In German: Schleifer)

This is an ornament of two, three, or, more rarely, four grace-notes which proceed by conjoint degrees, either from above or from below. The ancient sign for it was 𝆃 or ⁄ or \ placed *between* two principal notes.

The execution is the same as that of the double acciaccatura, i.e. rapidly and lightly. Its time-value is derived from the *following* principal note in the compositions of the older classics up to and including Haydn, Mozart and even Beethoven. There is this difference, however: Bach employed, at times, the *sign* of the slide, while the three great composers named never made use of it; they wrote out, instead, the notes as grace-notes.

Toccata in D Minor

JOHANN SEBASTIAN BACH

Sonata Op. 13 (Pathétique)

LUDWIG van BEETHOVEN

Although, as stated elsewhere in this chapter, Hans von Bülow, when writing about grace-notes never made reference to the *After-tones,* yet in this case he saw the necessity (in my opinion without absolute warrant) for allowing the grace-notes (the "slide") to be played as part of the preceding measure. Anent the foregoing measures von Bülow writes: "In executing this grace, the player must be careful not to produce the effect of parallel octaves with the bass (F-A♭, and in the next measure E♭-G); rather than this, the slide might be treated as an appendage to the fore-going notes."

There are other ancient signs, such as the "Accent" (designated thus by Bach); the "Port de Voix" (thus designated by Rameau, and similar to the "Accent"); the "Pincé" (an inverted mordent, considered by Rameau as a trill); the "Suspension"; the "Son Coupé"; the "Arpègement simple" and the "Arpègement figuré", all of them used by Rameau. I do not deem it necessary to speak of them at length because they have disappeared from general use. They will be found on the lists which I append as a curiosity. The first list is a table of signs written by J.S. Bach for his son Wilhelm Friedemann Bach, in his "Little Clavier-Book" (1720). The other list of signs is given by Rameau in his "Pièces de Clavecin, avec une table pour les agrémens" (1731 and 1736).

Those who are especially interested in this subject of musical ornamentation should consult the treatises devoted to Embellishments by Dannreuther, Ludwig Klee, Louis Arthur Russell, Beischlag, as well as the essays written in Grove's "Dictionary of Music and Musicians", and in Riemann's "Musik Lexikon."

Clavier — Büchlein
für
WILHELM FRIEDEMANN BACH
Angefangen in Cöthen den 22 Januar 1720

Explication unterschiedlicher Zeichen,
so gewisse *manieren* artig zu spielen, andeüten

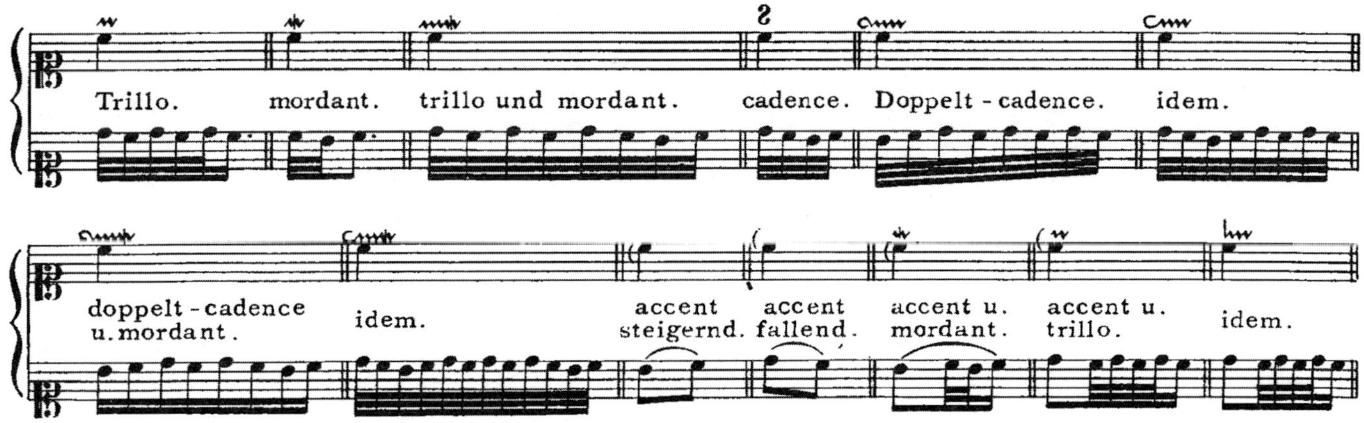

Pièces
De Clavecin
avec une table
Pour les Agrémens
par Monsieur Rameau

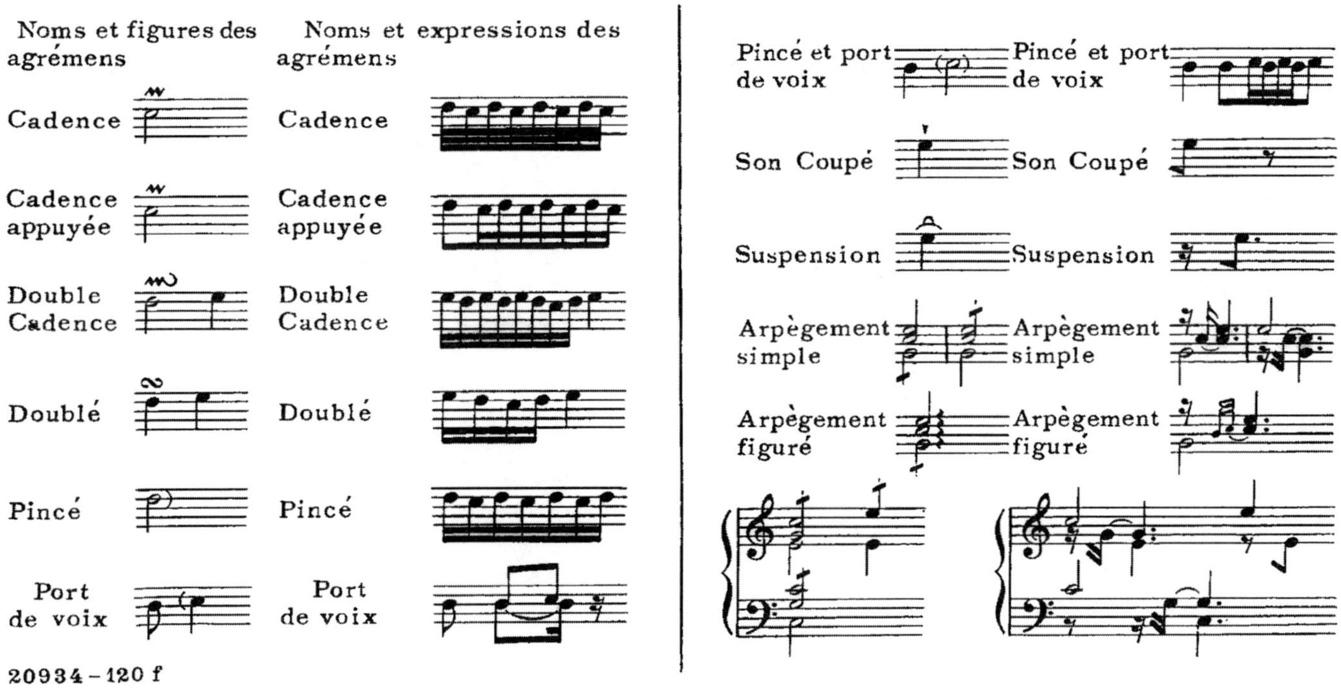

20934 - 120 f

Sight Reading

and

Pianoscript Book

Sight Reading

To neglect this valuable accomplishment is to burden one's life with a sense of incompleteness, of partial failure.

Time, energy and patience are wasted painfully deciphering music that should be performed at sight with nonchalant ease. For a poor sight-reader, learning new pieces is a task of far greater magnitude than for a good reader. The poor sight-reader rarely indulges in the delights of chamber music, and he cannot accompany at sight singers, violinists and cellists.

It has been observed that many good sight-readers have a poor or unreliable memory, while the musician gifted with a fine faithful memory does not read well at sight.

In 1801, Czerny began to take lessons from Beethoven. In 1805, Beethoven wrote him a brilliant certificate, but at the same time warned him not to make too free a use of his extraordinary memory "as he might otherwise lose the ability of a quick survey when reading at sight." (Thayer, "The Life of Beethoven," Book II.)

There is, however, no reason for not possessing both accomplishments. The artist who has slips of memory whenever he appears in concert is to be pitied still more than one who has failed to develop the faculty of reading well at sight.

All the advice, suggestions and rules ever given, and all that are given in this chapter, are contained in the following three words: Read every day.

Unless this is strictly adhered to, the poor sight-reader will not gain ultimate success.

Therefore, the first requisite is to be quite sure that no day passes without devoting from five to thirty minutes to sight-reading.

The best time for reading is either at noon, before the midday meal (the light is best then), or in the afternoon, before day light wanes. But if the pianist finds out by experience that in spite of personal desire and good-will he forgets to read at sight, or is prevented by other occupations, then he should read at sight in the morning, the moment he sits down at the piano.

If the first requisite for obtaining success as a sight-reader is to read every day, the second is to have suitable and plenty of music to read.

By suitable music is meant music easy enough to be read with fluency. Music of the so-called second grade is best to begin with. As the pianist gains more and more ability he should read music of third grade, fourth grade and so on; but nothing is more disheartening than to try to read at sight music difficult to *learn*.

Orchestral players are usually better sight-readers than pianists, for two reasons: first, they usually have only one note to play at a time, while the pianist has many; and they practise very little, if at all, while the pianist devotes to practice all the time he can dispose of.

The following points are worth remembering: do not start playing the moment the music is placed on the rack. Look carefully (but swiftly) at the clefs, number of accidentals, at the clef tonality, time-signature and tempo.

Read *silently* the first few measures and if given time, cast a careful but rapid look over the whole composition, or movement, in order to find out if repeats are to be made, if the tempo changes suddenly, or if the music suddenly becomes much more difficult than it is at the beginning. Then, after this preparation, start playing without anxiety, making up your mind to *enjoy* both the reading and the music, if it is beautiful. Pay no attention to slight, often unavoidable, imperfections in your reading or in your playing. You are not asked to play the music at sight perfectly, but to give as good a sketch of it as you can. Never stop, and never repeat a passage because you made one or two slight mistakes. If the music suddenly becomes difficult, play only the right hand part and the lowest note of the bass, or, if need be, leave the bass out altogether, picking it up again as soon as you are able to play well the parts of both hands. If the reading was very poor, do not repeat the piece immediately; read it again a couple of weeks later.

Do not stare at the music. In order to counteract that habit make it a *practice* to cast a *swift* look at a whole measure and immediately look away and play whatever you gathered in that one swift look. It will not be long before you find out that you can play two measures, possibly more, by glancing once at the music and then looking away from it. This will develop the habit of playing at sight, not by studying every note, as a child spells the letters of a word, but by obtaining a quick impression of whole groups of notes, as a well educated person takes in words, and even whole sentences, when reading a book.

When reading at sight *always play with shadings and expression and use the pedals;* you will, then, read better and enjoy your reading more.

Before you start your practice in the morning get ready the music which you mean to read later during the day.

Read at first only pieces in a slow tempo, not faster than *Moderato*. Later, when reading pieces in *Allegretto* or *Allegro*, play them in that tempo, and not slower, for you would get a wrong impression of the piece. It is highly beneficial to read polyphonic music at sight, such as the Little Preludes and Two and Three Part Inventions by Bach, his Partitas and his French and English Suites. The eye then becomes trained to read at the same time two, three, and four different parts.

If possible, arrange with a fellow-student, or with a friend, to read at sight, once or twice a week, symphonies arranged for four hands.

Begin with the Symphonies of Haydn; then Mendelssohn, Mozart, Schubert, Beethoven, Schumann, Tschaikowsky and Brahms. The list of beautiful Suites and pieces written originally for four hands, by Arensky, Grieg, Jensen, Raff and other eminent composers is very extensive.

Try also to play sonatas and pieces once or twice a week with a violinist or a cellist. This will prove profitable and delightful. To accompany singers is also of great value, as it gives the pianist the opportunity to play at sight music which is seldom very difficult technically but which requires instant adaptation to the various little dynamic and agogic changes that a singer generally indulges in.

Of course all this takes it for granted that the pianist has a good knowledge of harmony, which enables him to recognize at a glance not only the the category of chords but the chord-like structure of certain passages, the relation between the bass and the melody and the modulations.

When you have become a fairly good sight reader, try to organize every week, an evening or afternoon of chamber music, (trios, quartettes or quintettes). This is of great educational value and one of the purest joys of the real musician.

The Pianoscript Book

If mention is made here of this little book of mine, called Pianoscript Book, it is because of the undeniable help it has proven for both teacher and student. The fact that the Pianoscript Book is now in its fourth edition speaks more eloquently than words for its usefulness and widespread acceptance.

The Pianoscript Book is designed to retain, in classified form, the observations made by the teacher in regard to technic, position of hand, touch, tone, interpretation, defects to correct, qualities to acquire or to develop and so on-- all of which the student is usually told and promptly forgets.

The Pianoscript Book contains besides many technical exercises, brief instructions for using the pedals correctly, and numerous suggestions, rules and advice regarding the various phases of pianistic art.

In the belief that the Preface of the first edition of the Pianoscript Book, which is reproduced in all subsequent editions, gives a clear idea of its aim and scope, it is quoted herewith:

*) "Teaching is one of the most beautiful vocations to which any individual may devote himself. For, rising above our own short existence, we impart to others truths and principles which shape their minds and their very souls, gladdening and sweetening their lives. To the musician, teaching means gracing the days of his fellow beings with the beauty and fragrance of the masterworks in music. The joys and the sorrows, the aspirations and the force which stirred the great composers to create their immortal works glow anew when we perform their compositions. We and our pupils know how to conjure again to magic life the wondrous, vibrant tonal messages from the silent symbols.

"Yet the task at times is arduous! What a strain on the patience and the nerves of the teacher to have to repeat, over and over again, that which should be treasured at first hearing by the student! What a confession of carelessness and inattention it is when the pupil admits that he has forgotten what the master has said! The result of a life's experience, knowledge and investigation freely given by the teacher but forgotten in a moment by the pupil!

"In order to lighten and at the same time make more permanent the work of the master and of the student this book has been devised. The only student worth while is the thoughtful student. This book provides such a student with a practical means of preserving in classified form a record of his own work, observations of his master and his own comments upon the lessons. In other words, what has been hitherto kept in unstable form in the memory may now be preserved *for all future reference.*

"The result will be startling. What the teacher really has to give, beside his own illustrations at the keyboard, and which is of most value to his pupil, is his advice. Why try to keep it on the easily effaceable tablets of the mind?

"By keeping a careful record the pupil will then tread swiftly, smoothly and safely, that road which leads to the desired goal--to Knowledge, Mastery, Success."

Used in conjunction with the Master School, the Pianoscript Book is a powerful help for utilizing to the utmost the technical, musical and aesthetic material contained therein, thereby avoiding *stagnation* in an art where not to progress means to retrograde.

*) By permission of Theodore Presser, Philadelphia.

Conception

and

Interpretation

Conception and Interpretation

Some musicians may think that the words which head this chapter signify the same thing: the correct understanding of the meaning of a composition. There is, however, a distinction to be made.

Conception, as applied to the art of a musical performer, means his ability to understand correctly the nature, purpose and poetic idea of the composition which he is to play.

Interpretation is the performer's ability to actually reproduce his conception of the piece in a manner that approaches as nearly as possible to the composer's idea.

Conception is the idea which we form of the piece. Interpretation is the manner in which this idea is made audible.

Interpretation refers not only to our conception of the piece, but to our more or less correct, faithful, clever, intuitive or inspired translation of the musical signs written by the composer into living, vibrant tones.

To interpret well means to give to the tempos just the speed that the composer intended, to the shadings the greater or lesser intensity he had in mind, to the accentuation the firmness or moderation he wanted, to the touch the degree of buoyancy or mellowness in staccato or legato that he designed and thus, too, in regard to the agogics, to the employment of the pedals, to outlining the phrases, to the style, in short to all that goes into giving audible life to the silent symbols.

We may endow a piece with a beautiful conception and yet fail to interpret well or beautifully all that the composer wrote. There is a gift which may be developed, but which can neither be imparted to nor created on barren soil; it is a powerful means for interpreting a musical composition correctly and beautifully. This gift is called taste.

What is taste? I know of no better definition than that given, over one hundred and fifty years ago, by Jean-Jacques Rousseau:

"Of all natural gifts, *Taste* is the one which is felt most and which can be least explained. It would not be what it is if it could be defined, for it judges of matters over which our judgment has no control, and it serves, if I may so express myself, as spectacles to reason."

"There are melodies more agreeable than others although those others may be written equally well. From a harmonic standpoint, some compositions are effective and others are not, though all may be correctly written. There is the exquisite art of offsetting some compositions against others, which is based upon something more subtle than the law of contrasts. There are various ways of performing the same composition without departing from its character; and of these various ways, some are more pleasing than others, and not only is it impossible to submit such interpretations to rules, but it is even impossible to define them. Reader, tell me what these differences are and I shall tell you what Taste is.

"Each person has his own peculiar Taste by which he bestows upon those things which he calls beautiful an interpretation which belongs to him alone....

"In all cases, each person having but his own Taste to offset against that of another, it follows that none may dispute him.

"However, there is also a general Taste, to which all persons of good judgment readily submit, and that is the only kind of taste which can be defined absolutely as *Taste*.

"If this perfect unanimity does not exist, it is because all may not be equally sensitive; because all may not be persons of Taste, or because prejudices, either of habit or of education, are apt to change, through arbitrary convention, the appreciation of what is naturally beautiful. As for these various tastes, they cannot be disputed, because there is only one which is true, but I know of no other means of ending the argument, when tastes disagree, than that of counting the votes."

"Genius creates, but Taste chooses; and often a too prolific genius needs a severe censor who will prevent him from squandering his riches. Without Taste one may do great things; but it is Taste which makes them interesting. It is Taste which enables the composer to understand the ideas of the poet; it is Taste which enables the performer to understand the ideas of the composer; it is Taste which furnishes the one and other with that which may adorn and enrich his subject; and it is Taste which gives the listener the feeling of their mutual concord.

"Taste, however, is not to be regarded as synonymous with sensitiveness. It would seem that Taste concerns itself more readily with smaller forms, and sensitiveness with larger ones." ("Dictionnaire de Musique," by Jean-Jacques Rousseau, 1777).

Instrumental compositions may be classified as follows:-

1. Those that by their form give an unmistakable idea of their nature and meaning. To this class belong all dance music, marches, barcarolles (boat songs) and berceuses (cradle songs).

2. Those that bear a title, or motto, which indicates the character of the composition. This includes nocturnes, fantasy pieces with titles and also transcriptions of songs or of operas; more rarely, movements of sonatas and chamber music.

3. Those that having no title, no motto and no particular name, except a generic name, such as sonata, fantasy, ballade, scherzo, novelette, give by themselves no indication what the music is intended to portray. It is in this class of compositions that the performer needs all of his knowledge, imagination and intuition in order to read between the lines, that is to say, to sense and to understand what the composer strives to express.

If we examine the first class mentioned, we find that some dance music is meant for dancing, while some is not. A waltz by Johann Strauss is evidently meant for the ball room. The music is nearly always cheerful and graceful. No special conception and interpretation are needed here, except a conception of happiness and gaiety and an interpretation that is rhythmical and suited to dancing. All the concert transcriptions that have been made of Strauss' waltzes do not alter the original conception and interpretation of the waltz theme and are meant only as a display for technical virtuosity and brilliancy.

Not so with the waltzes of Chopin. He gave to the waltz a new and exalted position in music. The Chopin waltzes are not intended for dancing and it is indeed practically impossible to dance to them if they are played as they should be played.

In the Waltz in A minor, Op. 34, No. 2, what sadness and yearning in that opening slow theme in the left hand!

The two themes that follow in the right hand try to shake off this despondency; they leap forward, bespeak gaiety, cajole and then melt into a fourth theme, in A major, vibrant with love and passion.

But the fourth theme is repeated in the minor mode and it all returns to the first, slow melody in the left hand, so sad, so beautiful!

Another theme appears, still in the left hand. Again hope and love and happiness! Is this dance music! This is as fervent an appeal as ever welled up from the heart of a lover and it is answered now and then in vibrant, loving tones by a higher voice.

Again the first sad strains! And without a coda, just so, it all ends. Unhappy love, bewitchingly sung by an inspired poet. Who would want to play this as a waltz for people to dance? Such music stirs us all the more for being expressed in a form that usually is dedicated to gaiety and frivolity.

But not all the waltzes of Chopin are cast in this mould. With some of the others is coupled the gilded vision of aristocratic Parisian salons, dainty perfumes, beautiful women and courtly knights.

This is what conception may do with such an apparently innocuous form of music as the waltz. It finds a broader scope in the mazurkas and in the polonaises of Chopin. Love of Poland, the splendor of the nobles, the misery of the poor, suffering and strife--- all are depicted in them.

In the chapter on "Rhythm, Measure, Accents" it has been said that "there is no more striking illustration of the difference between mere 'keeping time' and an adequate rhythm than is offered by marches and march-like themes. They are not all alike in character and consequently the life, the nature of the rhythm, is not the same in each. That funeral marches are slow and stately and military marches quick and buoyant needs no demonstration. But there are subtle differences in each of these categories of marches, which are due to our conception of the piece."

This conception will influence the interpretation, that is to say, the whole manner of playing the composition.

In Grieg's "Ase's Tod" (The Death of Ase) we know that the composer depicts the death of Peer Gynt's aged mother. The mourner's steps are to be timed one for each quarter-note and two for each half-note. A sombre uniformity, a dull sorrow, enshrouds the whole composition. The mournful tread follows the hearse of a human being.

Ase's Death Op. 46, No. 2

EDVARD GRIEG

Andante doloroso (♩ = 50)

Not so in the third movement of Beethoven's Sonata, Op. 26, over which he wrote: "Marcia funebre sulla morte d'un eroe" (Funeral March for the Death of a Hero). This funeral march was written by Beethoven when he heard that Napoleon Bonaparte had had himself crowned Emperor of France. Beethoven had admired Bonaparte as a hero, the saviour of France. Now he saw him only as an *intrigant* who had done all for selfish ends, because of his lust for power. This Funeral March was written in memory of a man still living!

Marcia funebre sulla morte d'un eroe
Andante Maestoso (𝅗𝅥 = 68 - 72)

That it is of more heroic proportions than "Ase's Tod" every musician will acknowledge. It is, above all, orchestral, and the roll of the drums and the strident calls of the trumpets are heard therein.

Andante maestoso (𝅗𝅥 = 72 - 76)

With such a conception to guide us, the interpretation cannot go astray.

The thirteenth variation in Brahms' Variations on a Theme by Händel, is also a funeral march of a character akin to that of Beethoven. We have no clue as to what the composer had in mind, but of the heroic character of the funeral march there can be no doubt.

Variations and Fugue

on a theme by Händel

Var. XIII — JOHANNES BRAHMS

(Tempo di Marcia funebre — *(A.J.)* (♩ = 60)

In Chopin's well-known Funeral March, which is the third movement of his B♭ minor sonata, the canvas is still larger. This striking composition mourns not the death of any individual, but the death of a whole nation, Chopin's beloved Poland. The breadth and sweep of this masterpiece should inspire the pianist to interpret it in a manner befitting its lofty conception. This funeral march is unique, in this sense, as well as in others, that the funeral theme is followed by a marvelously beautiful melody provided with an entirely different rhythmical accompaniment. This melody is up-lifting, vibrant with hope, like a fervent prayer. It is an interlude in the funeral march proper and has, moreover, this characteristic, that it should be played a little more rapidly than the funeral march. The first theme returns, unchanged and the march ends without a coda. Here, the author of this work plays, in the three last measures, the left hand chord

an octave lower than written, whereby a muffled sonority and a gruesome effect is obtained, as of earth being thrown on a coffin. The effect is startling.

Of truly epic grandeur is the Funeral March written by Liszt, entitled "Funérailles". It commemorates a battle in which three of Liszt's dear friends fell. It is somber, harsh, broad in conception and intensely virile in design. The clash of arms is portrayed graphically and in a manner that suggests the brass instruments of the orchestra, the drums and the timpani.

Funerailles

FRANZ LISZT

It ranks with the Funeral Marches of Beethoven and Chopin, among the greatest ever written.

How different the rhythm, accentuation and general character, because the *conception* is so different, in Gounod's "Marche funèbre d'une Marionette" (Funeral March of a Doll)! A burlesque, a musical joke? Yes, and this knowledge, imparted by the title as well as by the flippant character of the music, will change the interpretation.

Funeral March of a Marionette *(Doll)*
CHARLES GOUNOD

Marches of other character also differ among themselves because their inner life and their rhythm influence our conception. Suffice it to compare the march of "Midsummer Night's Dream" by Mendelssohn with the march in "Lohengrin" by Wagner; with the "Kaiser March" by Wagner; with the "Marche Militaire Française", in the "Suite Algérienne" for two pianos, by Saint-Saëns; with the March for four hands by Beethoven.

If the sonatas and Fantasies for piano that bear a special title had not been given any, would we still know their significance? Supposing that the Beethoven Sonata Op. 81a, mentioned in the chapter on "Musical Prosody", had not been called "Les Adieux" (Farewell) by its author, would we still recognize in those three movements the departure, absence and return of a loved being? One may answer affirmatively. We would also grasp the meaning of the "Wanderer" Fantasy, Op. 15, by Schubert, which embodies the same idea of departure, absence and return. We would know the meaning of this composition, even if the word "Wanderer" had been left out.

In nearly all instances, however, it is only through the words which the composer has written at the beginning of his composition that we obtain a partial, at times complete, idea of its character: *Andante* of the Sonata in F minor, Op. 5 by Brahms; "Sea Pieces", by MacDowell, and so on).

Outside of his Sonatas Op. 81a and Op. 13 which he called "Pathétique" Beethoven gave no title to any of his sonatas. He never dubbed his Sonata Op. 27, No. 2, "Moonlight". This foolish and utterly unsuitable title was given by some publisher and unfortunately it has stuck ever since. Other titles have been bestowed by publishers on other sonatas of Beethoven which are not so inappropriate as that of "Moonlight". Thus, the Sonata Op. 28, in D major, is called "Pastorale" in several editions and there is no denying that the first and last movements convey the impression of quiet, country life. The Sonata Op. 53 is called "Aurore" in the Litolff edition and also in some French editions. In this instance it is the last movement only which gave birth to the name. The author of this work must acknowledge that he never played or heard played the opening measures of this last movement without receiving a vivid impression that it portrayed the dawn of day.

Sonata Op. 53

LUDWIG van BEETHOVEN

Rondo
Allegretto moderato (♩=108)

In the two last mentioned sonatas, both the conception and the fancied title bring about an interpretation more descriptive than emotional or psychological.

In Thayer's "Life of Beethoven", there is the interesting account which Czerny gives of the lessons he had with Beethoven. The following short quotation comes well within the frame of this chapter: "His interpretation of the scores by Händel and by Gluck, as well as of the Fugues of Bach, was incomparable. To the former he knew how to give a fullness to all the voices and to impart to them a spirit that gave to these compositions a new aspect."

Noteworthy also is what Czerny who, it should not be forgotten, was a highly esteemed pupil of Beethoven, writes in the third chapter of his "Kunst des Vortrags" (Art of Execution) on the mental conception of the compositions by Beethoven:

"When several good actors play the same rôle, for instance, "Hamlet", each interpretation will be different in many details. One will emphasize with great effect the melancholy, the other, the irony, a third, the simulated madness, and yet all these portrayals may be satisfactory, provided that the main conception is correct."

"Likewise, in the interpretation of classical compositions and especially those of Beethoven, much depends upon the individuality of the performer. One may emphasize the humor, the other, the earnestness, the third, the feeling, the fourth, the bravura; but he who knows how to combine them all is undoubtedly, the best interpreter."

Hans von Bülow, with his fine analytical mind and keen insight has given, in the foot-notes to his edition of the Beethoven sonatas, many striking proofs of how an accurate and poetic conception of a composition may beautify the manner in which it is played, that is to say, the interpretation. Suffice it to quote the following:

"The author's direction "*espressivo*" must not tempt to a sentimental conception or to a *tempo rubato*. The plaintive tone in the interval of the descending minor second must, on the contrary, be conceived humoristically, and the whole movement taken in a *tempo* as strictly uniform as possible." (This refers to the second movement of the Sonata Op. 54.)

"Imagine the first subject executed by wind-instruments -- say clarinets and bassoons; one measure before the second subject, the muted strings fall in, while oboe and flute alternately bear the melody." (Second movement of the Sonata Op. 79.)

"This closing refrain, or epilogue, may be played somewhat broader, as if accompanied by a deep breath, but in an even *ritenuto* rather than *rubato*. The closing measures should be whispered as modestly and simply as possible, i.e.: without any unfitting pathetic delay." (End of the first movement of the Sonata Op. 90).

"Resist the temptation to bring a *ritardando* at the close. The theme must vanish like a spectral vision." (End of the *Scherzo* of the Sonata Op. 106).

When a fanciful title is affixed to a short piece, such as the "Fantasy Pieces", Op. 12, by Schumann, the conception of the piece is, of course, indicated thereby. But in the larger forms a larger canvas confronts us and it is not always easy, nor is it given to everyone to form a just idea of the meaning of the composition. It is then, and especially in compositions where no clue is given, that an accurate and lofty conception based on *knowledge, imagination* and *intuition* determines the value and beauty of the interpretation.

Expression

Musical Prosody

and

Musical Declamation

Expression--Musical Prosody and Musical Declamation

The vocal expression of man may be classified as follows: Speech, Declamation (Oratory) and Song.

In ordinary conversation, the accents given on certain syllables and on certain words, the distinctness or strength with which consonants are pronounced and the inflexions as well as the range of the voice are all moderate. They become at once more marked when reading aloud, or when speaking in public; the principles of *prosody* or good *diction*, are then made manifest. The larger the audience, the stronger must become the accents which are bestowed on syllables and on words, the greater the distinctness in the pronunciation of consonants, the more impressive the inflections and the more forceful the emission of the voice.

Prosody and Diction are synonymous in their bearing upon a clear, well modulated speech.

No other requirements than those mentioned are needed if the speaker is dealing with subjects that have no especially appealing or emotional character. But if the text to be read aloud, or the address to be made to an audience is of such nature that it appeals to man's emotions, to his sympathy, pity, love, energy and resolve, or if it denounces and brands that which is abhorrent to us, in short, if it is of a poetic or dramatic nature, then a further change takes place in the speaker's mode of expression; his voice becomes more vibrant, its range extends, encompassing often an octave or even a tenth; his accents are more vehement; his gestures more sweeping and more assertive. He has reached the domain of *declamation*, the most stirring expression of speech to which man can rise and beyond which lies *Song*.

Musical Prosody

That there is speech in music, akin to language, must have been sensed by the man who first strove to express in music the feelings and emotions that welled up in his heart. The compositions of J. S. Bach, which to some persons, seem to be the outcome of a purely scholastic mind, offer countless examples of fervor and deep-felt emotion. Did Bach see in music more than problems of counterpoint? Read what Spitta, his best and most authoritative biographer, has to say: "But more important yet is it to know that the thought came to him of comparing piano playing with the speech of man. He could not have done this if, for him, music had not possessed a perfectly developed language of its own; if his many polyphonic pieces were not like unto the utterances of so many different human beings; if he had not considered a composer to be also in a sense, a dramatic poet." (Johann Sebastian Bach, by Spitta, Book I, page 666).

In the second movement of the sonata Op. 111, of his edition of the sonatas of Beethoven, Hans von Bülow uses the significant word "parlando" (speaking):

Von Bülow is yet more explicit in a foot-note to the sonata Op. 109: ".... the language of tones possesses a syntax quite analogous to that of words-- though unhappily not yet formulated in any text book."

As far as I know, this chapter constitutes the first attempt to investigate the possibility of Musical Prosody, to examine its affinity with the prosody of language as well as its role in music, and to find rules and give advice for its practical application in a pianistic performance.

In language, Prosody has for its province the clear, correct pronunciation of words, with special regard to the length of and emphasis to be laid on vowels; also the proper use of the cadences of the sentences. Similarly, Musical Prosody consists in giving to the notes of a melody the proper articulation, combined with the required accents, slight delays and dynamic and agogic nuances.

Musical Prosody is necessarily closely connected with phrasing, which teaches the construction of phrases and their interdependence and connection with each other; with musical form, this being the esthetic development of musical themes; with accentuation in its manifold forms; with dynamics and agogics, which bespeak tone and tempo nuances, similar to the inflections and the flow of the voice.

The accents of Musical Prosody are of especial significance. They depend not only on the phrasing, tempo and character of the music, but also on the performer's conception and the interpretation of the piece.

In language, a good observance of the requirements of prosody enables a person to speak distinctly, correctly with taste, and in accordance with the rules of grammar, of syntax and of the idiomatic characteristics of a language. Such a person will be listened to with attention and pleasure. Musical Prosody, likewise, enables a performer to deliver the notes of a *cantilena* in such manner that a clear, plastic and grateful impression is produced.

The affinity between prosody in language and prosody in music becomes manifest as soon as music is put to words. It is evident that the music should then preserve the necessary accentuation of certain syllables; yet this fundamental condition for a beautiful blending of language and music is often neglected by composers; great composers at times have failed in this respect.

"Even the greatest composers are sometimes not sufficiently attentive to the accentuation of the words which they set to music. For instance, in the following passage from 'Freischütz' Weber has, by means of syncopation and a *sforzando,* thrown a strong stress on the second syllable of the words 'Augen' 'taugen' and 'holden' all of which (as those who know German will be aware) are accented on the first syllable.

"The charm of the music makes the hearer overlook the absurdity of the mispronunciation; but it none the less exists, and is referred to not in depreciation of Weber, but as by no means a solitary instance of the want of attention which even the greatest masters have sometimes given to this point." (Grove's Dictionary of Music and Musicians).

In contrast to the above, Thayer, in his "The life of Ludwig van Beethoven", writes: "The sketches of the greater part of Beethoven's songs after the Bonn period are preserved and prove with what extreme care he wrought out his melodies. The sketchbook analysed by Nottebohm affords a curious illustration in Matthison's 'Opferlied,' the melody being written out in full not less than six times, the theme in substance remaining unchanged. Absolute correctness of accent, emphasis, rhythm -- of prosody, in short, -- was with him a leading object; and various papers as well as the Conversation Books attest his familiarity with metrical signs and his scrupulous obedience to metrical laws."

In the chapter on "Phrasing" it has been said that the words of a song help a singer to phrase correctly. They also help him to give the proper prosodical accentuation. Therefore, one of the best ways for a pianist to learn to play with a due regard to Musical Prosody is to study song transcriptions for piano. Those by Liszt are particularly grateful: "Auf Flügel des Gesanges" (Mendelssohn-Liszt): "Hark! Hark the Lark: (Schubert-Liszt); "The Erl King" Schubert-Liszt); and "Dedication" (Schumann-Liszt).

Schindler, pupil and friend of Beethoven, in whose house he lived for several years has left it on record that, "For the *Cantilena* (melody), Beethoven gave as an example well-trained singers who neither exaggerate nor restrain themselves unduly. He advised further to occasionally couple suitable words to certain melodic passages and to sing them, or to hear such passages played by a well-schooled violinist, or a player of wind instruments".

The Romance in E♭ Major by Rubinstein, was first written as a song and later transcribed for piano by Rubinstein himself. By comparing the original song with the Romance, a pianist will be able to see on which notes of the melody special accents are due, and in which manner the melody should be "said." This applies also to "Ich liebe dich" (I love thee) by Grieg, written first as a song and then transcribed for piano by the author.

One should know not only what to do but also what to avoid.

If in a song (of which a piano transcription has been made) accents are given on words that should not be accented, the effect will be ludicrous, and the whole meaning of the words may be changed. Apply these wrong accents to the transcriptions for piano, and you will realize how they pervert the musical prosody of the phrase.

Another instance of the value of prosodical accents is found in the introduction of the Sonata Op. 81a by Beethoven. On the three opening double notes, Beethoven wrote "Lebewohl" ("Fare thee well"):

Should these syllables be played entirely without accent? To do so would hardly convey the impassioned speech of one who laments the departure of a person whom he loves. Then, if an accent *is* necessary, where should it be placed? Certainly not on the middle word, "thee." If a marked accent is given to the last word, "well," it expresses a wish for a contented, almost jolly, state of mind on the part of the one who stays, wholly incompatible with these words of love, longing and regret. Therefore, a slight accent should be placed on the *first* word, "fare."

Although Schumann did not write the word "Warum?" (Why?) over any of the notes of the lovely composition that bears that name, (Fantasy Pieces, Op. 12) it is easy to see where the word would fit:

As in German the accent falls on the second syllable, it follows that the second note should also be slightly accented.

Practical Rules and Advices

Unless otherwise prescribed by the composer and provided that their time value is not too short, the higher notes of a group of melodic notes are to be accented more (by emphasis or delay) than the lower notes. The highest note usually receives the strongest accent or a slight delay and is to be considered as the melodic culmination.

Nocturne Op. 9, No. 2
FREDERICK CHOPIN

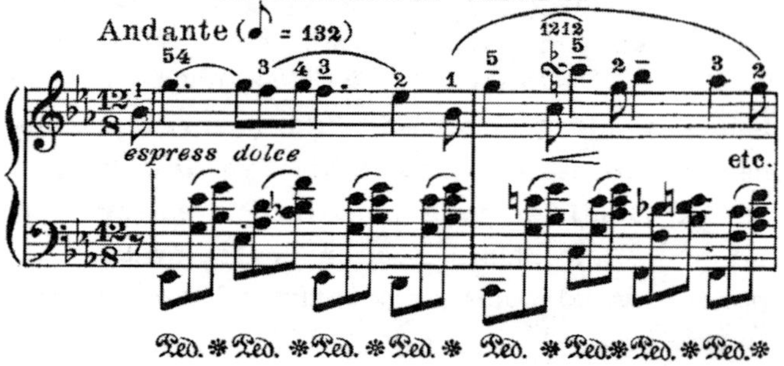

As a general rule, the longer the duration of a note, the stronger should be the prosodical accent.

Passacaglia in C Minor, of J. S. Bach
arranged by Eugène d'Albert

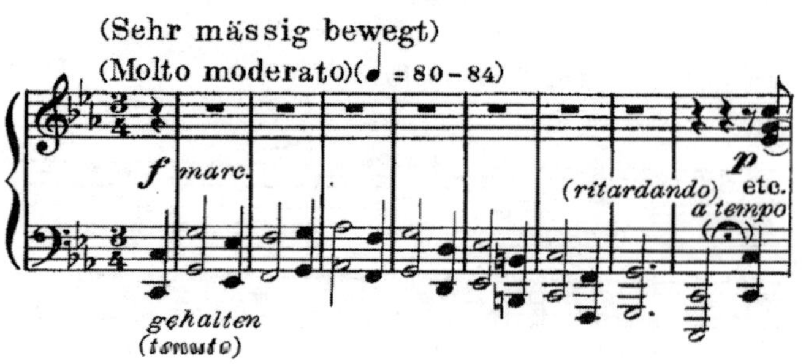

The prosodical accentuation of vowels and the distinct enunciation of consonants find their counterpart in music.

In the following example, the dotted eighth notes may be likened to vowels; the sixteenth notes to consonants. These should be clearly articulated, but the emphasis, that is to say, the prosodical accent, is due on the dotted eighth notes, corresponding to the beats of the measure.

The Greek word *thesis* means "down-beat." This down-beat, unless otherwise indicated, receives the strongest accent. The thesis occurs on the first beat of measures in duple and triple time ($^2/_4$ and $^3/_4$ and their derivatives). It also occurs on the first beat of $^4/_4$ time in a rapid tempo. But in a slow tempo, a less marked accent is often due on the third beat.

In opposition to the *thesis* the Greek called *arsis* (the up-beat) the unaccented part of the measure. (See Riemann's Musik Lexikon).

Sonata Op. 26
LUDWIG van BEETHOVEN

Andante con Variazioni (♪ = 80)

Symphony No. 3 (Eroica)
LUDWIG van BEETHOVEN

It should be noted how insipid and even confusing the last example would sound if played without this natural accent of the *thesis*.

The importance of a prosodical accent on the first beat of the measure has been recognized by many celebrated virtuosos. Says Grove: "The famous instrumentalists of the classical school, such as Joachim, Mme. Schumann, Sir Charles and Lady Hallé, Piatti, and many others, were accustomed to mark the natural accent, as distinguished from emphasis, not by enforcing the sound, but by a hardly perceptible prolongation of the first note of the bar."

Appoggiaturas invariably take the accent from the following note. (See the chapters on "Rhythm-Measure- Accents" and "Embellishments").

It has been shown in those chapters that in our modern way of writing music, the appoggitura often appears in disguise, but that it, nevertheless, keeps the accent. As an appoggiatura appears always a half step or a full step above, or below, the note to which it is coupled, it follows that it rests with the composer, or the performer, to determine which note should assume the role of appoggiatura.

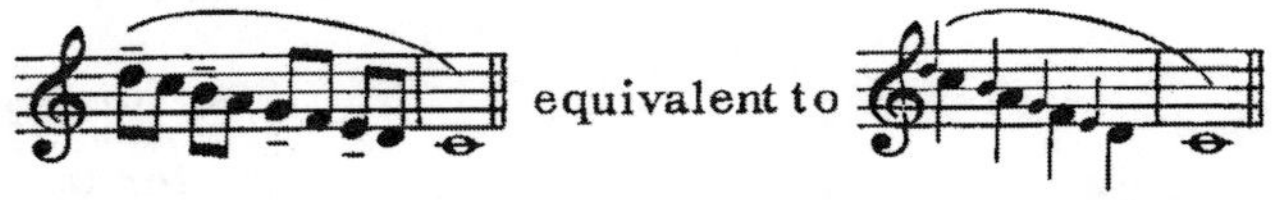

The "natural" accents fall always on the beats (especially on the so-called strong beats) of a measure. But from the standpoint of musical prosody, the accent, delay, or intensification may occur anywhere.

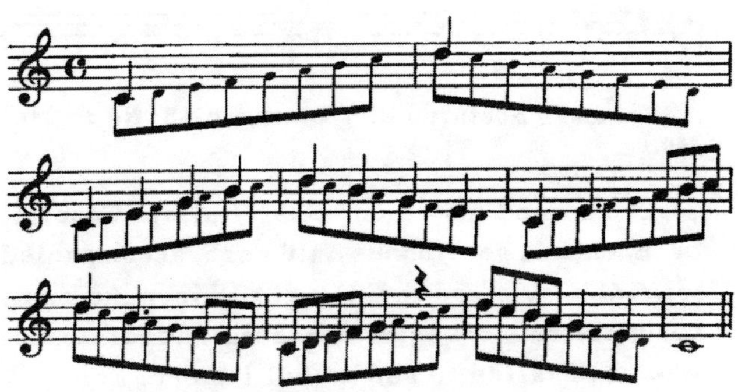

In contradistinction to natural accent is *syncopation* which requires a special accent (see the chapter on "Accents").

Reviewing what has been said we find that, from the standpoint of musical prosody, the notes of a melody may be divided into notes on which a certain accent or repose is due (vowels); passing notes (consonants); syncopations; appoggiaturas, (notes to "lean upon"); notes on which there must be a special prosodical accent.

Plagal and perfect cadences (especially the latter) convey a feeling of "finality." This should be emphasized like a dynamic or a melodic culmination, by a more or less marked ritard on the last note or chord.

Just as prosody, or good diction, are the fundamental requisites for the most stirring expression of language:- Declamation, or Oratory, so an intelligent understanding of Musical Prosody enables a musician to grasp the full meaning of Musical Declamation.

Musical Declamation

In language, declamation means an exalted, poetic intensification of the voice which dramatizes the text by greater vibrancy of tone and of accents, with a more extended compass of the voice and with more emphatic and more sweeping gestures.

In music, a similar intensity of expression takes place when the rendition of the *cantilena* demands an impassioned delivery.

The principles and rules that govern the Musical Prosody apply also to Musical Declamation. Hence, it is necessary to illustrate here only the meaning and effect of declamation as applied to music.

In the main, the need of musical declamation is felt in only three phases or forms of the musical speech; in *cantilena*, or melody, when it assumes a highly dramatic character; in *recitativo*, or monologue; and in dialogue.

Of the first form the following quotations may serve as fitting examples. In some instances, even though provided with an accompaniment the melody has a recitative character.

Symphonic Variations
for piano and orchestra
CESAR FRANCK

(See also: Nocturne in C minor, Op. 48, No. 1; Melody, from Gluck's "Orpheus," arranged for piano by Sgambati, etc.)

The second movement of the Italian Concerto, by Bach, is a continuous, although accompanied, *recitativo*. Viewed in this light, this wondrously beautiful music becomes understandable to those who have failed to get its full import.

The *recitativo* proper has no accompaniment. It partakes of the character of a chanted speech, and of a spoken melody. It is the bridge between speech and song.

"*Recitativo*. A discourse recited in a musical and harmonious tone. It is a method of singing which approaches nearly to speech, a declamation in music, in which the musician should imitate, as much as possible, the inflections of the declaiming voice." ("Dictionnaire de Musique", by Jean-Jacques Rousseau, English Translation by William Waring - 1779).

The greatest, most beautiful *recitativos* written for the piano are found in the compositions of Bach and of Beethoven. Witness those in the Chromatic Fantasy and Fugue, by Bach. What grandeur, what pathos is expressed in them! At times methinks the old Greek chorus is evoked here, for such must have been the impassioned recitation of the ancient psalmodist as he sang and was answered at intervals, in short, wailing, or fiery accents by the surrounding chorus of singers. "The Grecian tragedy was at first nothing but a chorus of singers"--(Dryden). Or is it the Jewish chant which is heard here--this strange melopoeia, with its trills, turns and shakings of the voice, at times lamenting, anon querulously supplicating, a blending of the old Arabian, Egyptian and Hebrew priestly invocations-- and which to this day are sung in the synagogue by the high-voiced Rabbi?

Chromatic Fantasy and Fugue
JOHANN SEBASTIAN BACH
(Hans von Bülow edition)

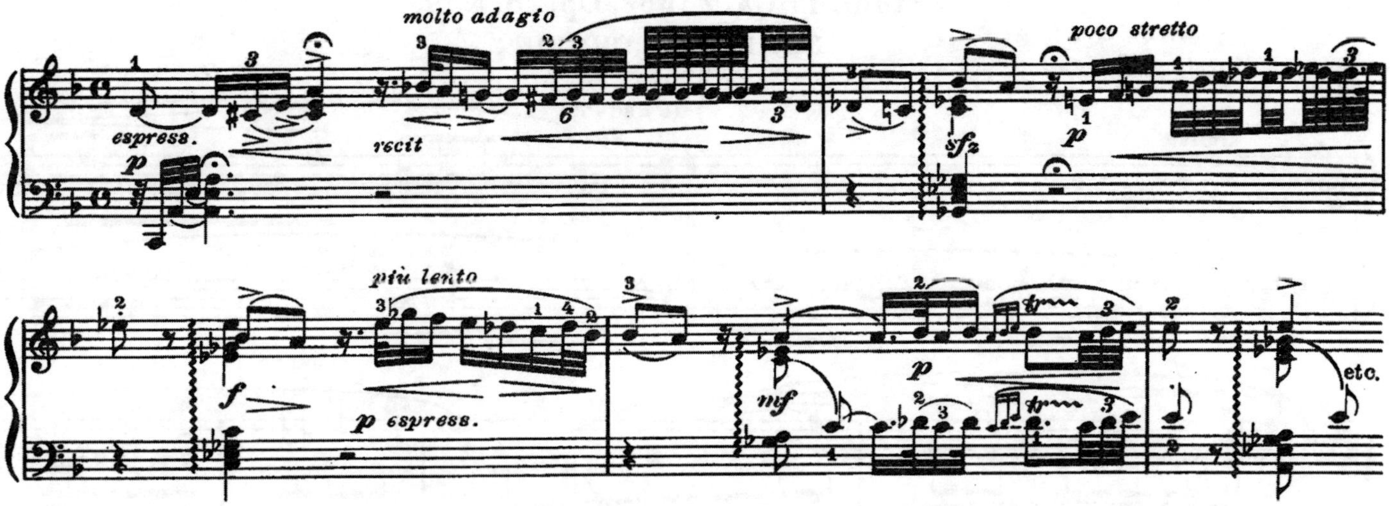

The recitatives in Beethoven's sonatas have a more pathetic, more poignant character than those of Bach. The immense mind that gave them shape, the great soul from which they sprang into existence, sang and wrote of the joys and sorrows of mankind, of its aspirations, love and faith, and lost illusions with a peculiar force of dramatic expression.

Sonata Op. 31, No. 2
LUDWIG van BEETHOVEN
(Hans von Bülow edition)

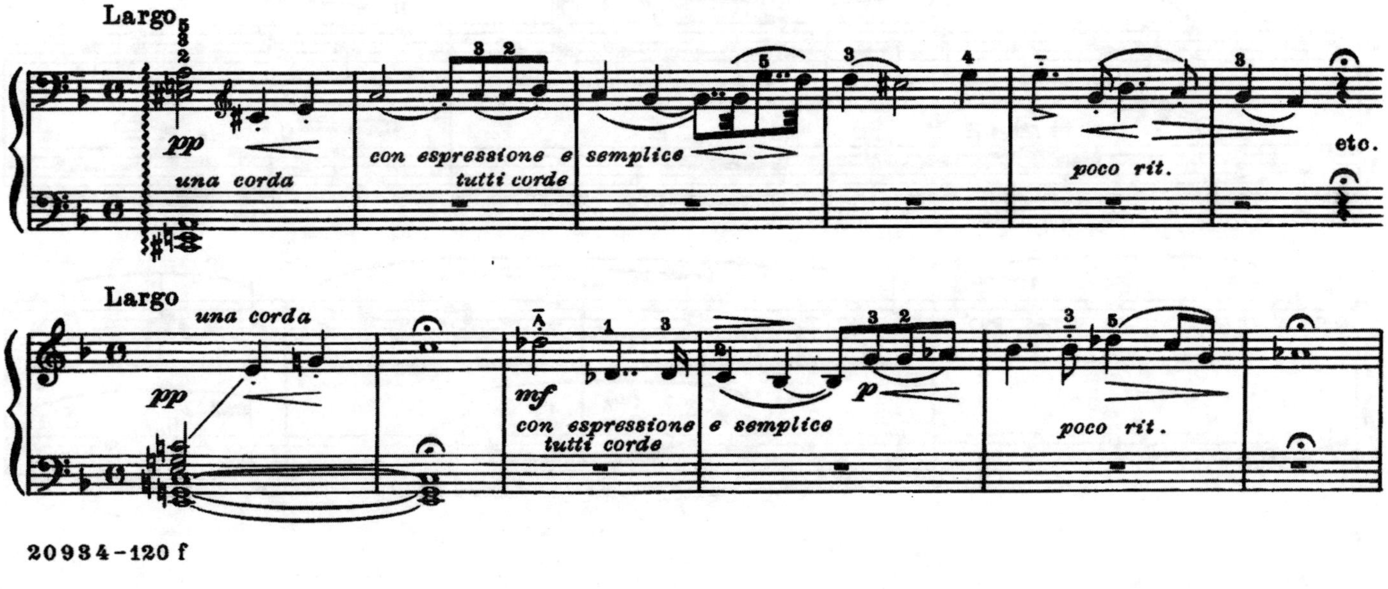

In language, a dialogue is a conversation between two persons and this conversation may be of a placid nature or not. In music, the term "dialogue" is applied to the simul - taneous, or alternating, execution of two "voices" or parts, the music being of a poetical or dramatic character. A dialogue is usually a duet in which love is expressed in tones of sad, yearning or ardent passion. The declamation should then mould itself after the impassioned speech or song of two lovers, the lower part like the voice of a man, being brought out with a fuller, heavier sonority and with less nim - bleness of articulation, while the upper part, like the voice of a woman, is made to sound more ethereal, more slight of volume and of greater nimbleness in articulation.

Etude in C♯ Minor, Op. 25, No. 7

FREDERICK CHOPIN

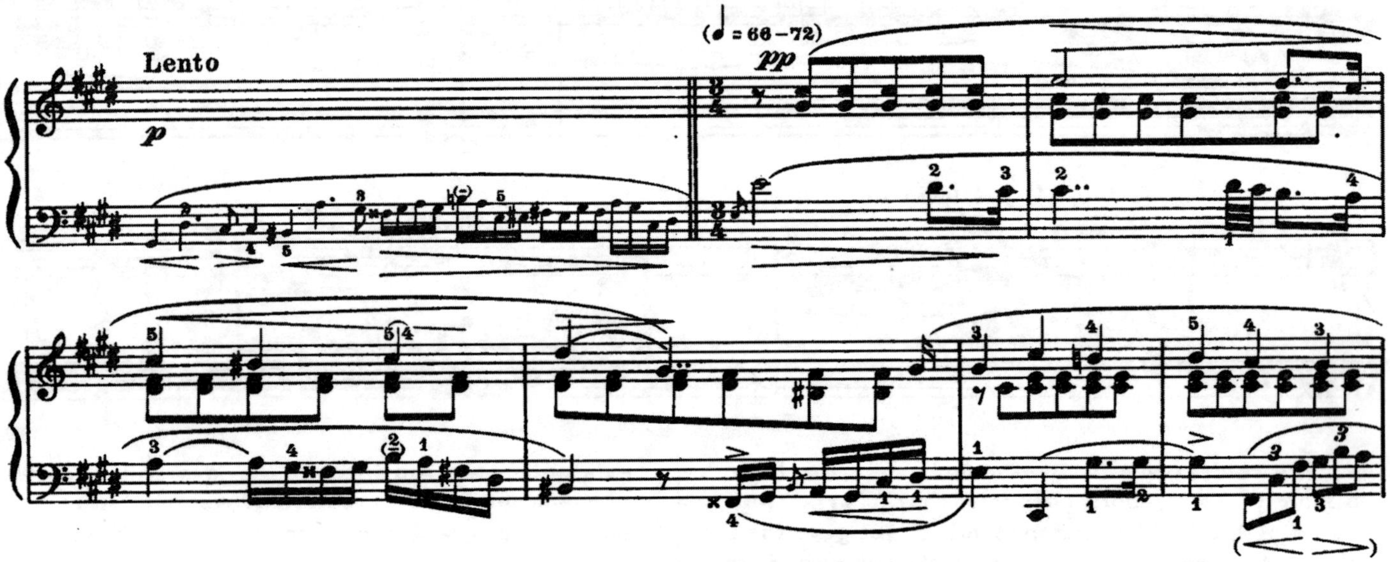

Polonaise in C♯ Minor, Op. 26, No. 1

FREDERICK CHOPIN

In the foot-notes of his edition of Beethoven's sonatas, Hans von Bülow often, and feelingly, bespeaks the need of musical declamation:

"Here," writes von Bülow, "piano-playing ceases; whoever is unable to lend soulful "speech" to his instrument, should content himself with reading." (Adagio Sostenuto, Sonata Op. 106.)

Of the following passage in Beethoven's sonata Op. 81a, 1st movement, von Bülow writes: "A beautiful and effective interpretation of this dialogue cannot be taught."

Allegro (𝅗𝅥 = 120) (Hans von Bülow edition)

And in a foot-note to the second movement of the same sonata, we find the following:-

"These last six measures of transition to the Finale rank among the most ingenious and emotional of the composer's "fancies." The grief of the sorrower at the absence of the loved one has been uttered in a plaintive monologue, then a moment of unconsciousness supervenes, wherewith is interwoven a mute, subtle premonition of the other's near return. It is as if one could see the lonely one wandering with eyes fixed on the ground, when the features are suddenly illumined; a lifting of the eyes, an exclamation of ecstacy, an impatient hastening to meet the returning one. Another composer might perhaps paint with more striking and variegated colors, but certainly not more plastically, warmly and delicately. In this last movement the monologue is supplanted by one of the most ecstatic of musical dialogues, rivalled only by that in Richard Wagner's "Tristan and Isolde" (Act II, scene 2).

Interesting also is the advice given by Beethoven and transmitted to us by Schindler: "Just as the poet keeps his monologue or dialogue within a certain unbroken rhythm, and yet the declaimer, in order to insure the understanding of the meaning, makes shorter and longer pauses even in such places where the poet could not indicate any punctuation signs, similarly may this art of the declaimer be used in music."

In his "The life of Beethoven"---the first biography of Beethoven ever written--- Schindler, speaking of Beethoven's art of declamation mentions that he used the caesura and the rhetorical pause, both derived from Clementi; also points of rest, even when the composer did not expressly indicate them."

Schindler quotes the C minor Sonata Op. 10, from measure thirteen to measure twenty-one in which are to be found these rhetorical pauses. They are described by Schindler as follows: "The abruptly terminated phrase is to be played impetuously and to the written rests of quarter notes in the upper voice are to be added two more quarter note rests; the idea being to increase the suspense."

Musical Prosody! The art of "speaking" in musical tones in a correct manner, adequate to the text to be "read".

Musical Declamation! The command over all the eloquent means by which the inner spirit and glow of music are revealed.

Yet--both prosody and declamation are but the vehicle for that which is the very soul of music: Expression.

Expression

For an artist it is rather surprising and disconcerting to have a pupil ask him, as often happens, "Do you want me to play my piece with expression?" The pupil might as well ask whether he should let sorrow make him sad and happiness make him gay.

The reason for this and similar questions is to be found in a misconception of the word "expression." It is often used by the pupil (and also, I regret to say, by the teacher) when the word "shading" is meant.

There is a great difference between shading and expression.

Expression nearly always includes shading. But shading a piece may be accomplished without bringing to light the purpose, character, mood, spirit or atmosphere of the piece; without investing it with the personal equation of the player -- *his own* feelings, emotions and thoughts which he, both unconsciously as well as through volition, sets in tune with the thoughts, emotions and feelings which swayed the composer as he created his work.

Unconscious Shading

Shading a piece may be accomplished through a purely mechanical process, or by reason only; usually it is though, by an unconscious process that our feelings dictate the distribution of lights and shadows, of *fortes* and *pianos, crescendos* and *diminuendos*. Shadings correspond to the heaviness or lightness of the drawing; to the intensity of the color applied to the painting. Shadings may, therefore, be considered synonymous with the greater or lesser volume and intensity of a sound.

But expression is all that the music has awakened within us, whether directly or indirectly connected with the music.

Just as we perceive an object because a greater or lesser part of the rays that strike it are reflected to us, so *expression* is the reflection of the *impression* made on us by a tone poem and which we project from our own personality. But in order that the projection - this expression--may take place, our impressions must have been keen and strong. The deeper and stronger and keener these impressions have been, the more potently and convincingly will they be projected from ourselves through the medium of the instrument.

Therefore, the first requisite for acquiring the power of expression to a marked degree, is a rightly endowed artistic nature which can contribute something further than a highly developed technic and glittering brilliancy.

He who would express must have feeling--in the true, deep and lovable sense of the word; a responsive heart; warm blood coursing through his veins; unselfishness, depth and constancy. He must understand the composer's intentions and be both willing and able to give them anew audible life.

He must possess and carefully safeguard a musically sensitive nature. This includes sensitiveness of the musical ear, which perceives the slightest difference and fluctuation in the pitch, volume and color, or *timbre*, of the sound; sensitiveness of feeling for harmony, in its blending of consonant and dissonant sounds; sensitiveness as to the slightest change in the tempo, so that once the tempo of a piece is heard it is never forgotten; sensitiveness to the *rhythm* and to the measure; sensitiveness to accentuation, touch, delicacy, strength, and, above all these, to the inner, glowing life of the composition, to its appeal to the intellectual faculties or to the emotions of man.

Expression has always been considered as the highest and noblest aim of both the composer and the performer. The following significant words were written in the time of the clavichord and clavicembalo:-

"As a musician cannot move others without himself feeling emotion, he must be able to arouse in himself all the emotions which he would impart to his hearers; he makes them understand his feelings and can in this way best excite them to sympathy........ This becomes more especially his duty in pieces of an expressive cast...... in playing which he must feel the same emotions that moved the composer when penning his composition".

"It is to be observed that, as a rule, dissonances are to be played louder and consonances more weakly, because the first emphasize the emotions and the latter quiet them." ("Essay on the true method of playing the Clavier", by Carl Philipp Emanuel Bach, 1753).

Of greater scope and vibrant with eloquence is the essay on "Expression" given by Jean-Jacques Rousseau, in his "Dictionnaire de Musique" (1777). It should be read thoughtfully by every aspiring musician.

"Expression. A gift which enables the musician to feel keenly, to render in a decided manner all the ideas which he is asked to impart, and all the sentiments which he is asked to express. There is the expression of the composition itself, and the expression of the performer, and it is from their happy union that the most musical and most agreeable effects are obtained."

"Our speech is diversely colored according to the various emotions which affect it -- now sharp and vehement, now careless and irresolute, then again varied and impetuous, or even and tranquil. From this source, the musician derives the differences in the modes of his song and the pitch at which he must sustain it: either causing it to issue from the lower register of the voice at small intervals, to express the heaviness and dejection of sorrow, or from the upper range, to express sharp sounds of excitement and grief, carrying him rapidly through the entire range of his scale in the agitation of despair or the violence of contrasted emotions. Above all, we must particularly observe, that the charm of music does not consist in mere imitation, but in an agreeable imitation, and that declamation must be subordinate to melody, so that one cannot depict a sentiment without giving it a certain secret charm which is intrinsic, nor touch the heart without pleasing the ear. And this is comformable to nature, which gives the voice of sensitive persons certain penetrating and delightful inflections which are not accorded to persons of unemotional nature. Therefore, do not confound rant with expression, nor harshness with energy, nor give an ugly portrayal of emotions which you are to express.

"The quantitative value of words when coupled to the notes becomes nearly lost; and music instead of expressing itself in words, uses the measure, which is a language in itself. The power of expression consists, in this connection, to reunite both languages as much as possible, so that if measure and rhythm do not speak in the same language, at least, they will say the same thing."

"Gaiety which lends vivacity to all our movements, must impart vivacity to the measure; sorrow, which cramps the heart and retards our movements, must similarly affect the song which it inspires; but when grief is intense, or when great conflicts take place in the soul, speech becomes uneven, alternating between the slowness of the spondaic and the rapidity of the pyrrhic, or it may cease abruptly as in the case of Recitatives. It is for this reason, that the most expressive compositions, or at least, the most impassioned, are usually those wherein the time-values, although equal to each other, are the most unequally divided, whereas sleep, rest, peace of soul, are readily portrayed by equal time-values, which move neither rapidly nor slowly."

"It is vain for the composer to imbue his work with that warmth which must be present in it, if this is not transmitted by the executant. The singer who sees in his score nothing but notes, is not qualified to comprehend the expression of the composer, nor to give expression to his song. One must understand what one reads in order to make it comprehensible to others and it does not merely suffice to be sensitive in a general way, if one cannot be so with respect to the eloquence of the language one speaks."

"Do as you would if you were simultaneously a poet, a composer, an actor and a singer, and you will give all the expression that is possible to give to that composition which you must render."

Ferdinand Ries was one of the few pupils whom Beethoven accepted. Ries studied with Beethoven for several years and was the first pianist to make his public debut as an accredited pupil of Beethoven. In the written description of his "Lectionen" Ries says the following: When I missed something in a passage or when I struck wrong notes or missed skips, even those that he wanted to be emphasized, he seldom said anything, but when I showed myself deficient in *expression*, in *crescendos*, or in the knowledge of the *character* of the piece, he became angry because, as he said, the first-mentioned mishaps were an accident, but the lack of expression showed lack of *knowledge*, of *feeling*, or of *attention*.

In Thayer's "The Life of Beethoven" is found a description which Friedrich Nisle, a composer, wrote of his visit to Beethoven. This description was published in the "Berliner Allgemeine Musik Zeitung", 1829. "They tell me that Beethoven has in Vienna pupils who play better than he does. This makes me smile. It is true that in the matter of *elegance* and *technical qualities*, others have excelled him; also, that on account of his hard hearing he played somewhat roughly. But these blemishes did not disturb one when the Master disclosed the innermost depths of his being. And how can *fashion* and *technical ability* (which is often nothing but mere finger dexterity) compensate for the absence of the soul of a Beethoven?"

Expressing is Creating

To express means to reproduce, with the inevitable admixture of our own individuality. To express may also be said to create anew.

The moment we read, play or sing, or hear a piece sung or played, we receive an impression; and it is hence forth impossible for us to play or sing this piece without investing it with expression of some kind. This expression will be more marked if we perform it often, or hear it sung or played often, and also according to the amount of freedom which we give to the impressions which the piece has produced on us. If we deny them admission, if we stifle them, we run great risk of deadening or obliterating entirely from our consciousness the effect made on us. Therefore, if we wait for a special grand occasion on which we are to play a piece "with expression" we may find only dryness and barrenness where the little, delicate blue flower of poetry was beginning to grow.

Play "with expression" the moment you begin to play at all. As your impression of the piece becomes more varied and deeper, your expression will likewise be richer, deeper and broader. As new points of view are disclosed by studying the piece, playing it over and over, *thinking about it*, so new effects, new vibrant strings will seemingly be added to the instrument and under your fingers evoke the magic life which is slumbering in the silent symbols.

Shadings alone -- no matter how skilful the dynamic treatment -- are insufficient to render adequately the magnificent, broad sweep of the following measures, which like the huge portico of a cathedral, admit us to a tone-creation of vast and noble dimensions; it is the Fantasy and Fugue in G minor of Johann Sebastian Bach, arranged for piano in masterly fashion by Franz Liszt. Something is needed here besides a firm touch, forceful accentuation, careful shading and skilful pedalling; the understanding of and capacity for reproducing -- for *portraying* --- the grandeur of this broadly conceived work.

The Fantasy and Fugue in G minor were written by Bach for the organ, and we can well understand that when incorporating therein the wealth of his musical ideas, he was influenced and helped by the infinite resources of the mightiest of all instruments.

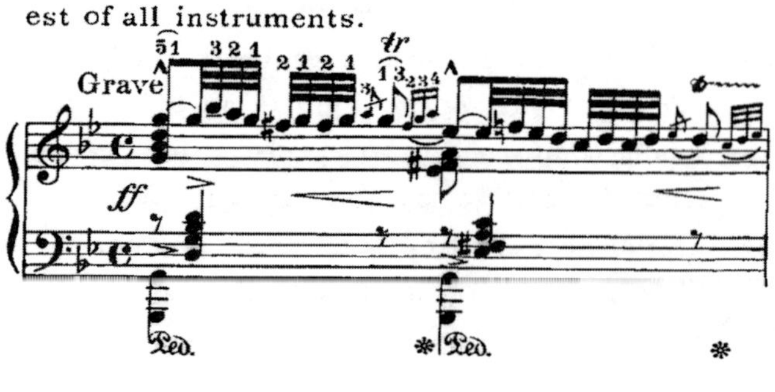

But what shall be said of the Chromatic Fantasy and Fugue, this wonderful example of tonal architecture, the fitting companion of the Fantasy and Fugue in G minor, over which it towers perhaps, through its boldness and vastness of design and the cyclopean strength of its execution?

The Chromatic Fantasy and Fugue, of Bach, remains in some respects an unsolved problem. Is it not wonderful to reflect that the great German wrote for the tiny clavichord a work that tests and exhausts the depth of tone and the power of our modern piano? The piano, the organ, the orchestra, the chorus, all seem to be needed here for an expressive rendition of this great work. (See above).

And how can shadings alone bring home to our hearts the fervent song of earthly renunciation, of heavenly hope, which Beethoven has sung in the second and last movement of the last sonata which he wrote for his cherished instrument.

To express well you must not only learn to speak well; you must *want* to express.

A Hindrance to Artistic Expression

We have seen the correlation of *impression* and *expression*. There is now one factor which may mar and destroy altogether, both in woman and in man, the gift of expression. This is *repression*.

Women, more than men, are taught in youth to repress their feelings, to preserve an outward composure in all circumstances, to curb the natural desire for venting their feelings in a forcible manner. This repression is, undoubtedly, necessary in everyday life, but it is fatal to expression in music, for here instead of hiding our feelings we are asked to bring them forth in as convincing a manner as possible.

"What then", might well be asked, "should be done? Shall a young girl, or a young man, just because he or she is musical and is studying music, be denied the fruits of a refined education, which certainly includes a certain curbing and repression in the *outward show* of our feelings when they are the result of annoyance, anger, repulsion, or even of joy? Should they be encouraged to loudly thump the table, while shouting with laughter in a public place, just because they are preparing themselves for a musical career?" The answer is evident. It is not, however, in the general education and the acquisition of deportment that the reason for the lack of expression in both men and women is found, but in the fact that the principles which govern deportment and general behavior are carried to the study room, to the piano on which we are asked not to *repress* but to *express* ourselves. Here full freedom should be granted. Purity, love, ardor, passion, sorrow, joy, despair, energy, faith, all should be interpreted with only such restraint as are dictated by good taste, by aesthetic reasons.

Thus the gift and power of expression, without detriment to personal refinement, will be cultivated and allowed to grow in early childhood and in youth--that is to say in the years when character is formed, when impressions are *strongest*, and when consequently, the power of expression, if cultivated, will soon be rooted deeply, bringing forth, in after years, the fragrant flower of personal charm, when interpreting on our beloved instrument the wondrous message left to us by the great masters in music.

Execution

and

Rendition

Execution and Rendition

Just as the words "Conception" and "Interpretation," which head the previous chapter, seem, at first, to be synonymous, although there is a vital difference between them, so the words "Execution" and "Rendition" may seem to some musicians to have the same meaning. Yet there is a decided difference.

Execution is the summing up of all the *pianistic* and *musical* qualities of the performer.

Rendition, or presentation, is the *personal manner* in which a musical composition is played.

The execution may be correct, even remarkable, and yet the auditors may not be enthused. perhaps not even interested, because the rendition was faulty or uninteresting.

Let us examine more closely these two subjects, among the highest of the pianist's art.

Execution

One may have a fine conception of the composition, one may feel how should be interpreted all that the composer wrote and even that which he did not, could not, actually put down on paper; that is to say, one may know how to read between the lines, and yet, like the would-be poet who claims to have wonderful poetic ideas, but who does not know how to write them, one may be unable to *play* the piece as the mind visualizes it. One is then unable to command a correct execution.

A mediocre pianist may, through intuition, *interpret* rightly, perhaps even beautifully, a difficult work (this, however, is an extremely rare occurence), but he will be unable to *play* it as he hears it in his mind. Nor will he, in all likelihood, be able to explain to others *how* to execute it, since he cannot do it himself.

Therefore, execution, while implying conception and interpretation, refers to the ability of the pianist to actually perform all that he wishes to play.

A flawless, brilliant execution means that the pianist possesses a beautiful, varied touch and tone; a highly developed and accurate technic; good rhythm; an effective and varied manner of accenting; a fine command over dynamics and agogics, in their manifold and most subtle "nuances"; that he knows how to "sing" on the piano; that he phrases correctly and uses the pedals with skill; finally, that his conception of the piece is correct, and his interpretation and expression are beautiful.

The execution, whether brilliant, forceful or delicate should, above all, appear "easy," unconstrained; in other words, the pianist should convey the impression that what he does is done easily, without undue physical effort and at times, with positive abandon.

What constitutes brilliancy? It is not easy to define it; it is as difficult to explain as "tact", "personality" and "atmosphere." Yet I shall try to define them all, since all are needed for an ideally beautiful performance.

For a pianist, brilliancy is obtained primarily by "articulation." This word means that every note of his scales, arpeggios and passage-work is made to stand out distinctly. It is obtained by a certain nimble action and strength of fingers (through stroke or pressure) given out in such manner that the notes of the scales, arpeggios and passage-work do not melt or blur into each other, but *stand out*, just as a public speaker, in order to be heard by a large audience, gives greater strength and distinctness to the consonants of every word he utters. (See the chapter on "Musical Prosody and Musical Declamation").

Hurrying slightly and "flaring up" all crescendos; giving zest and piquancy to all notes to be played staccato; using often the "jeu perlé" (pearly touch), (see the chapter on "Touch, Tone, Quality"); giving special care to the accentuation, (see the chapter on "Rhythm, Measure, Accents") using the pedals only when they create or heighten an effect -- all this will contribute to give to the playing that special glitter, forcefulness and sweep that makes a performance "brilliant".

As to the impression of "ease", of a masterful dominion over the technical difficulties, it will never be conveyed to an audience by the pianist who has "trouble" with difficult passages. "The thoughts and the feelings of the pianist, his whole musical nature and artistic inspiration would be as if laden with chains, should his fingers not be trained to their task and not be capable of conquering, without effort, the technical difficulties of the execution." (Guide du Jeune Pianiste, by Eschmann-Dumur).

Facilitations

In many cases this lack of technical mastery of a passage is not due to a lack of the necessary technical equipment, but either to poor fingerings, which the pianist persists in using (See Book V, the chapter on Fingerings"), or to the fact that the passage in question is not well written for the piano. In the latter case, even an accomplished pianist should not hesitate to facilitate a passage by distributing it between both hands whenever possible, or by other devices that enable him, without changing the text or the style of the piece to obtain an easier execution. In Book IV, page **91**, it has been said: "One should not think that facilitating a passage of extreme technical difficulty, or which does not lie well for the hands, denotes a lack of reverence for the great composers. Beethoven's style of writing for the piano is decidedly orchestral, and this is the reason why many a passage in his piano compositions is awkward of execution. It requires knowledge and tact to determine when such facilitations may be adopted without altering the euphony and the color, or the spirit and the style of a composition." The musical examples given there, on page **92** and **94**, should be studied.

I quote also from Book II, page **292**: "Always facilitate a troublesome passage, if thereby you acquire greater technical surety, without changing the text, or without interfering with its style. These facilitations are generally obtained by playing passages that are too difficult or are poorly written for one hand, with both hands in alternation. Such passages abound in the classical works written for piano, and are found with special frequency in the piano works of Beethoven. Never hesitate to use those facilitations, wherever they are really needed; you will appreciate this on the day of performance, when facing the public." The musical examples given there, (pages **292** and **293**) should also be practised. They may be supplemented by the following facilitations, which have been adopted by some of the greatest living piano virtuosos.

Etude in C♯ Minor, Op. 10, No. 4

FREDERICK CHOPIN

Better thus:

Rhapsody No. 6

FRANZ LISZT

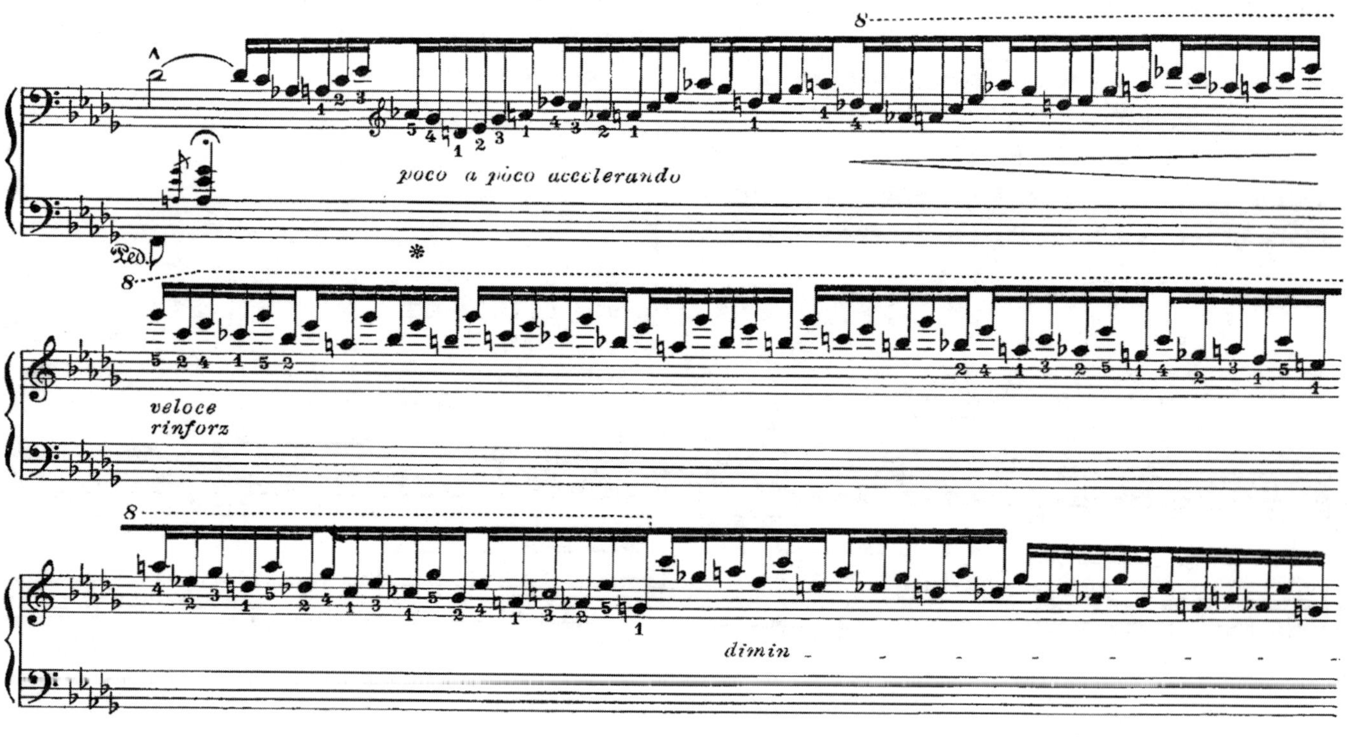

Better thus:

Sonata Op. 106

LUDWIG van BEETHOVEN

"This alternation of the hands prescribed in the original, though very convenient at the beginning in executing this passage, is fully as inconvenient at its close; the Editor therefore prefers to let the right hand run up uninterruptedly to the final note." (Hans von Bülow, in his edition of the Beethoven sonatas).

If any further proof were needed that a performer is, *at times* justified in facilitating a passage, the following excerpt from a letter written by Carl Maria von Weber to the music director Präger, in Leipzig, would furnish it.

"In the passage work, one should be mindful not to spoil the whole effect of the piece, because of any given run. For instance, he who cannot perform the last passages of the *Eglantine* with passionate fire, should facilitate those passages, rather than run the risk of diminishing the warmth and passion of the whole piece."

Repeats

There is a question on which many a pianist has sought enlightenment: Should signs of repeat be always observed? And if one is justified, at times, to disregard them, when may this be done?

The sign of :‖ or ‖: occurs more frequently in sonatas than elsewhere.

In the second chapter of his "Kunst des Vortrags" (Art of Execution) Czerny writes: "In the execution of the works of Beethoven (as well as in all classical compositions) the performer must make no change, no additions and must not shorten them."

Commenting on this passage, Franz Kullak, in 1881, wrote: "The general value of this sentence can hardly be disputed. Nevertheless, the omission of the signs of repeats in familiar sonatas and pieces of chamber music should not be considered as blameworthy exceptions."

One might draw the conclusion that it should be left to the performer's personal taste and inclination to repeat, or not, when the sign of repeat is indicated by :‖ ; but that when the composer writes 1ª (prima) and 2ª (seconda) the performer is bound to follow these indications.

Yet even here, notable virtuosos have disregarded the expressed wish of some of the greatest composers.

In a foot-note to the third movement of the sonata Op. 81a, in his edition of the Beethoven sonatas, Hans von Bülow writes: "There exists no aesthetic or formal necessity for the traditional repetition of the first part. That one may like to play it or hear it over again is no argument; for then one might just as well repeat it several times."

Hans von Bülow expresses himself still more forcefully in a foot-note to the third movement of the Sonata Op. 57 (Appassionata): "Excepting the case in the Finale of the C minor Symphony (first part), the Editor knows no more unjustifiable compulsion to repetition than this. The whole poem presses to a close; the player who thus far has striven with all the technical and mental energy at his command to fulfill his task, must now be so near exhaustion that it will take his entire remaining strength to meet the demands of the Coda—demands hardly to be over-estimated. If he obeys the repeat sign, his work will be inferior to the first time (unless he has been unduly sparing with his strength before); on the listener the repetition may make a didactic, but in no case an artistic impression; therefore, reverence, which the pianist accords even to intrinsic faults in the Master's works, might better be saved up for private practice, in which the interpretative musician must always be able to accomplish at least twice as much as is required of him at a public concert."

One must admire the courage of von Bülow in publishing these words which advise the striking out of eight measures written by Beethoven, the more so as many an artist felt that this should be done yet dared not say so or do so.

The passage cited by von Bülow is not an isolated one; many other instances may be cited. In my opinion the "prima" in the Scherzo in B minor by Chopin (measures 65-68) should be disregarded. No repeat should be made there.

But what a lack of artistic judgment would be evidenced if a pianist failed to make every repeat indicated by Beethoven in the second (and last) movement of his Sonata Op. 111!

The following suggestions will be found helpful: If the movement or part thereof is short, repeat it; if it is long you need not repeat it. If it begins on the tonic and ends on the tonic (of the same key) one will, generally, find that to repeat is irksome; but if it begins or ends on the dominant, or for that matter on any other degree of the scale except the tonic, or if it ends in another key, to repeat will not seem unpleasant.

One feels more like making a repeat if the music is cheerful, graceful and in a moderate or in a lively tempo; but when the music is mournful and the tempo very slow, to repeat is usually distasteful.

It is best not to repeat when the music is of such a highly dramatic or passionate character that, as in the case of the "Appassionata" (cited above) the performer runs the risk of either not being able to heighten the effect at the repeat, or of saving himself unduly the first time.

Finally, I refer the reader to the Chapter on Dynamics, in which the advice of Carl Philipp Emanuel Bach is quoted, regarding the advisability of varying the playing when repeats are made. Likewise to my advice, which I deem worth stating here again: if the music is loud, play it louder at the repeat; if it is soft, play it softer the second time.

Additions and Embellishments

Many a musician may think that there is no need to even touch upon this subject, because no one has a right to add to or alter what the great composers have written.

And yet there are instances where slight changes are not only permissible but at times imperative.

The clavichords and clavicembalos (harpsichords) and the early pianos had not the range of our modern pianos. This is the reason why in some of the compositions by Beethoven, scales or passages in octaves, in the bass, are abruptly terminated in single notes; his instrument went no further. In many such instances we are warranted in adding the lower notes (which his instrument had not) and in playing the whole passage in octaves. (See excerpt from Sonata in C major, Op. 2, by Beethoven, Book V page 62.)

This lack of range was undoubtedly the reason why some of Beethoven's themes have an entirely changed outline when they reappear in a high register of the keyboard; here, also, his instrument lacked the requisite range. But nowadays these shortcomings encountered by Beethoven are nonexistent, thanks to the enlarged range of the modern piano.

Sonata Op. 110

LUDWIG van BEETHOVEN

Moderato cantabile molto espressivo (♩ = 69)

"The incomprehensible descent of the spirited ascending figure on the third beat, as given in the Original Edition, may be explained (like some analogous incongruities in Op. 111) by a mere external circumstance. While engaged in composing these last piano sonatas, the Master used a grand piano furnished him by the London firm of Broadwood, the compass of which extended contra-C only to C^4, its extension downward beyond the Vienna pianos being made up for by an equally considerable loss above. Now-although it cannot be denied that the Master's lofty genius transformed every limitation of the means of representation at his disposal into a well-spring of new and characteristic beauties and refinements - we occasionally meet with cases wherein these limitations, which since then have succumbed to mechanical improvements, exercised a disturbing and disfiguring influence on the poetic intention. A proper discrimination of such cases is precisely the task of reverend criticism".(Hans von Bülow, in his edition of the sonatas of Beethoven, English translation from Schirmer edition).

A pianist is also warranted in slightly modifying the musical text when his hands are too small to play the chords written. The average hand can *reach* a tenth, but it is something else to *strike* tenths and chords of the tenth with ease and freedom, especially if the tempo is lively. Many great pianists can play only the ninth with freedom and assurance. Then if chords of tenth have to be played, it is permissible to play the written chord arpeggiated or with both hands or replace it by a chord that the hand can compass.

With the exception of his Sonata Op.106, Beethoven hardly ever employed chords of the tenth in his piano compositions. But in the *Adagio* of this sonata, he writes no less than *twenty-three* chords of the tenth. In the last four measures of the *Adagio* these chords of the tenth assume a special, highly esthetic and poetic significance. In their respective editions of the sonatas of Beethoven both von Bülow and d'Albert urge the pianist "to do his utmost not to arpeggiate these chords", except the last chord, with which the *Adagio* ends and to which Beethoven affixed an arpeggio sign.

Sonata Op. 106
(Grosse Sonate für das Hammer-Klavier)
LUDWIG van BEETHOVEN
Adagio sostenuto (♪= 92)
Appassionato e con molto sentimento

It seems evident, therefore, that Beethoven wanted all the chords struck like full chords, excepting the very last chord which is to be arpeggiated with the utmost delicacy. But Czerny has left it on record (see Thayer's "The Life of Beethoven", Book II) that "he (Beethoven) could hardly reach a tenth". If this was true, how did Beethoven play all these twenty-three chords? He evidently wrote them, taking it for granted that those who could not strike the chords would arpeggiate them. We should bear in mind that the keys of those early pianos (the sonata Op. 106 is the *first* sonata that Beethoven wrote for the then newly invented "Hammerklavier") were narrower than those of the modern piano. Nowadays the keys of the pianos of German and French make are a little narrower than most of those of American make, with the result that a pianist has to stretch less and can play more easily on those instruments.

But, reverting to chords of the tenth, and especially to these peculiarly significant closing chords of the Adagio in Op. 106, what shall a pianist do who, notwithstanding the admonition of both von Bülow and d'Albert, *cannot* encompass these chords and strike them as full chords? He is then compelled to arpeggiate them, or to employ both hands, which latter procedure he can apply in the third and fourth measure before the end.

Adagio sostenuto (♪= 92)
Appassionato e con molto sentimento

As to the chords in the last measure but one, the best advice I can offer is to substitute for them the following chords, or to arpeggiate them *note against note* (very rapidly and softly) while the very last chord is to be arpeggiated from the lowest note upward:

Other changes, made for the sake of greater brilliancy (they are not to be regarded as "facilitations") which have obtained the sanction of many of the greatest piano virtuosos and which appear printed in some of the foremost editions, consist in playing as full octaves, with alternating hands, passages written originally in broken octaves. Likewise, runs written originally as single-finger chromatics are played with alternating octaves.

Scherzo in B Minor
FREDERICK CHOPIN

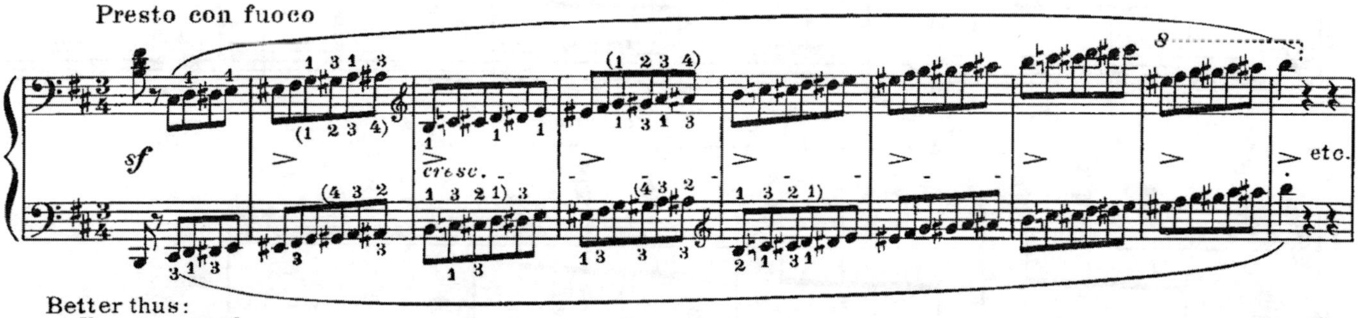

Better thus:

Scherzo in C♯ Minor
FREDERICK CHOPIN

Presto con fuoco (𝅗𝅥. = 104)

Better thus:

Concerto in E Minor
FREDERICK CHOPIN

Rondo
Vivace (𝅘𝅥 = 104)

Better thus:

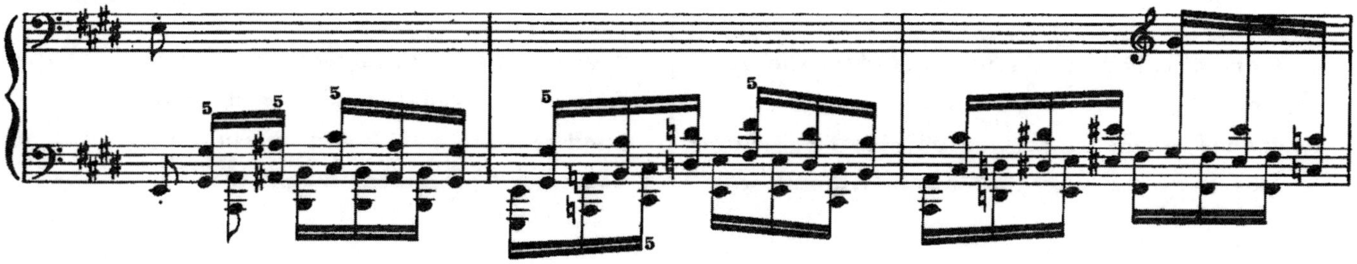

From what has been said the student should not draw the erroneous conclusion that he is free to change, whenever he pleases, what the great composers wrote. Facilitations, addition of octaves in the bass, as well as any other change from the original should be made only for justified reasons and should obtain the approval of competent, prominent musicians.

Rendition

The rendition of a musical composition is closely connected with, and depends on, the conception, interpretation and expression with which it is played.

Rendition concerns itself with the performer's personal style of playing; with his facial expression, gestures and deportment, with his reserve or his temperament; with his coldness or the warmth and fire which he displays; with his ability, or lack of it, to awaken and keep up the interest of his auditors, to kindle their enthusiasm by communicating to them his own enthusiasm; with his gift, if he has it, to make the listeners understand what he has to say (if he has anything to say!) and to make them feel the emotions which sway him.

The first requisite-- one that will command attention-- for a fine rendition, is personality.

There are two kinds of personalities; the outer and the inner. When the inner personalty is strong enough, it is always shown in the outer personality. We can not look at the face of Bach, of Beethoven, of Rubinstein, Liszt, Velazquez, Rembrandt, Victor Hugo, Goethe, Charles Dickens, Napoléon, Abraham Lincoln and a host of men whose achievements make their names stand out in history, without being immediately impressed by the intellectual force which their faces reveal. We would realize this force even if we knew nothing about them.

At times, though, the appearance belies the inner nature. Many a fair face, lit up by an ingratiating, even a bewitching, smile hides a cold, envious, selfish and unfaithful heart; many a plain-looking person gives to the superficial observer no outward indication of the wealth of lovable feelings, of the constancy, devotion and strength of character hidden within. As a rule, though, an intelligent man looks intelligent.

It is the inner personality that gives shape to ideas and feelings and translates them into a work of art; that gives to the eye the sparkle of enthusiasm, the suffused softness and depth of a generous, or the cold glitter of the worthless nature. It is the inner personality that enables the true artist to rise, as a performer, to *the same height* reached by the composer and not only to interpret him aright, but *to speak for him* in a manner that, whatever the import of the message, is sympathetic and carries conviction. "Nothing is so contagious as enthusiasm.... Enthusiasm is the genius of sincerity." (Edward Bulwer Lytton).

The outer personality is evidently the first to attract our attention. The wisdom of the proverb: "All is not gold that glitters" has been recognized in all countries. The first impression made on us by the face, expression and demeanor of a person may be favorable or not; subsequent knowledge of that person may confirm or reject the first impression by making us acquainted with the true, inner personality. On the concert stage the personal appearance, that is to say, the outer personality of an artist may at once win sympathy or command attention because of his impressive features, or it may count against him, but the moment he begins to play he finds himself speaking, in musical tones, to his audience. He should then, as already mentioned, have something to say and he should know how to say it in a manner that awakens interest, impresses, moves, and finally no matter what his looks are, compels the admiration and enthusiasm of his listeners.

Individuality is not synonymous with personality; it designates certain personal traits, a certain manner of speaking, acting, or playing that stamps what that person says or does or plays with a character all of its own.

Individuality begets *originality*, and if both are governed by taste, they become strong assets for artistic success; if taste is absent, these individual characteristics and the attendant originality degenerate into eccentricity.

Personality and individuality in their valuable sense are the outcome of strong inner convictions, of a really artistic nature, of a true, well-founded artistic faith, and of a constant striving towards high ideals. If these inner forces and graces are allowed to germinate and to grow under the guidance of a master-hand, or, as in the exceptional cases of Chopin and of Liszt, by the light of one's own genius, they will unfailingly blossom into a strong, commanding personality, which in turn will weave the magic spell called *magnetism*.

In order that this personality and this magnetism, besides being well marked, be also sympathetic, and even lovable, other requisites are necessary. The first is tact.

Tact may be defined as the instinct or intuition of knowing when and how to speak and act appropriately and when to forbear from speech or action.

A person gifted with tact does the right thing at the right time; he never offends through lack of consideration for other people's feelings, through a selfishness that blinds him to what is due others. For the pianist, tact prevents "pounding", exaggeration of all effects, as well as gestures, and a deportment not in keeping with the music performed. Tact, therefore, includes, or presumes, taste.

Through intonation and attitude, it is possible to offend a person by saying "Good day". Similarly, in music, a wrong manner of "saying" a piece, that is to say, a wrong rendition, may change its meaning or mar the effect.

As an illustration, let us suppose that a pianist while playing a funeral march nods or smiles at somebody in the audience. He would, obviously, be guilty of very poor taste and lack of tact, and his "rendition" would be very bad, no matter how fine his execution might be. Similarly, if a pianist while playing an entrancing, cheerful waltz assumes a sad facial expression, his rendition would be wholly inadequate.

It follows then that energetic accents require some proper emphatic gesture of the performer; that delicacy is not "rendered" well, unless the attitude and gestures of the pianist help the auditor to visualize as well as hear, the ethereal effects sought after; that music which is quiet and dreamy, cannot be "rendered" well with vehement motions, these being however, fully warranted in passages of passionate intensity and dramatic power.

This manner of emphasizing the character of the music by means of gesture or attitude may be called "display". This "display" of accents, or of fire and energy, or of a quiet, pensive mood, should be employed only when it helps to *portray* the music, and it should always be governed by taste and tact. It should never be so marked as to divert the attention of the auditor from the music. The display - attitude and gestures - should be to the music what the emphasis, attitude and gestures of a great orator are to his speech.

The truth of the above was not only felt but advocated in no uncertain terms by such an authority as Carl Philipp Emanuel Bach in his remarkable "Versuch über die wahre Art das Clavier zu spielen" (Essay on the true manner of playing the clavichord), published in 1753:

........"That all this may be accomplished without any gestures will be mantained only by those whose unemotionality makes them sit at the piano like a wooden statue.

Just as inappropriate or ugly gestures are disagreeable and unwarranted, so are good ones commendable, for they help to convey our intentions to the auditors. These inadequate interpreters do little justice even to fine compositions, no matter how perfect their execution may be. They seem not to know the meaning of these compositions, since they cannot portray it. But let them listen to the playing of one who has warmth of feeling and who possesses a good rendition! They will then be astonished to find that those compositions contained more than they knew or imagined. This proves that a good rendition may make acceptable and successful even a mediocre composition.

"Versuch über die wahre Art das Clavier zu spielen"
Carl Philipp Emanuel Bach

The following quotation is likewise of great interest, and be it remembered that all biographers agree that Beethoven's manner of playing the piano was extremely fiery and impressive:

"Beethoven's attitude while playing was masterfully quiet, noble and beautiful, without the slightest grimace"(Thayer's "Life of Beethoven". Book II).

There are still a few considerations left which deserve our attention.

A performer who shows timidity and embarrassment will never convince or enthuse his hearers, for the first requisites for impressing the auditor are confidence and authority.

And this does not mean a bumptious, overbearing attitude.

It means that the performer must give the impression that he is fully qualified, both technically and musically, to appear before an audience. This authority can and should, be coupled with a modest behaviour.

An audience will never be impressed with the rendition of a performer whose whole attention seems directed to a clean execution of the piece. Such generally happens with those who learn a new piece shortly before the concert. Their playing then lacks the assurance and abandon which are the outcome of a sufficiently long study and especially of having played it in public repeatedly.

To create the "atmosphere" of the piece is one of the most difficult and most artistic accomplishments. "Visions of nocturnal, quiet beauty, peaceful moon-lit landscapes; the slow rocking of the boat under the starlit sky; the nodding slumber of flowers; mothers dreaming at the cradle of their child; the impressive hour of twilight; up-lifted, silent prayers from sorrowful hearts--these arise before our mind when the soft pedal, enhanced through a beautiful, delicate touch, itself inspired by a generous heart and a poetical mind, raises the magic curtain behind which dwell the happiness and joy music can give". (Quoted from the Chapter on "The Artistic Employment of the Piano Pedals", Book VI).

Perhaps some of my readers might feel like asking, "How can this be accomplished? How can one create atmosphere"?"

Nothing but the playing of an artist endowed with a poetical, *creative* mind who knows how to surround whatever he plays with the proper "atmosphere" will be of help to him.

One will soon notice that deliberation and poise, or fire and impetuosity, or a quiet, absorbed demeanor go hand in hand with the character of the music. Yet this does not quite explain it, for hovering over the execution and the demeanor is the indescribable something--possibly the soul of the artist--that tinges a musical composition with the subtle life and light it needs.

It would be futile to try to give rules for "rendering" a musical composition correctly and beautifully. The analysis, suggestions and hints given so far, supplemented by the following parting advice, must suffice:

The attitude of the performer should be unconstrained, quiet, and thoughtful. Absolute immobility is, at times-- but for a short time only-- a powerful means for riveting the attention of an audience. It should be followed by greater freedom of motion. During the delivery of his song, a singer often rises on tiptoe, extends his arms, turns his body to left or right, sways slightly, steps a little forward or backwards; in short, acts in the manner of a speaker who addresses an audience. A violinist also indulges, whenever necessary, in this freedom of movement.

The pianist, who has already the disadvantage of not being able to face his audience, and whose profile only is seen by four fifths of the audience, is further handicapped by having to remain seated while he plays. It is evident that when it comes to moments of intense declamation, of personal appeal, he possesses less means than the singer or the violinist.

Yet, there remains to his disposal several motions of the body which he can and should employ with *tact* and *discretion* as occasion demands. He may lean to the left, to the right, forward and backward. He may also draw himself up, or even rise slightly from his seat, when emphatic accents are required.

At no time, however, should the demeanor and the gestures of the pianist be such that by centering on them, continuously and exclusively, the attention of the audience, they overshadow the music itself. Between the *artist* who yields, in a measure, to the emotions which the music arouses in him, and the mere performer who indulges in eccentricities is a wide gulf.

It is only to him, the worthy interpreter, that the reflections, suggestions and advice embodied in this chapter are dedicated.

Style

Style

The style of a composer stamps his musical creations with the same individuality that an author gives to his literary productions. Buffon said "Style is the man". Chesterfield gives the following definition: "Style is the dress of thought". Flaubert's *dictum* was: "Le mot juste", (The right word).

All this finds its counterpart in music.

Under the caption "Style", I have now in mind not the manner and deportment of a pianist while playing a piece (this is to be considered as the pianist's personal style of playing the piano -- see the chapters on "Rendition" and also Successful Playing in Public"). I have in mind his ability to do justice to the characteristics or peculiarities of the composer and of the period in which the composition was written.

In a vague, general way every student knows that a composition of Bach should not be performed in the same manner, or to be more precise and correct, in the same style, as a composition by Chopin or by a modern composer. Wherein lies the difference? It is for the purpose of defining and thoroughly understanding the difference between the styles of the great composers that this chapter has been written.

The Early Clavichordists

The early composers wrote for the *clavichord* and *clavicembalo* (in English, *harpsichord*) when these instruments were in their "infancy", so to speak; when they had not yet acquired the full development and means of expression that enabled later a Rameau, a Domenico Scarlatti, a Händel, a Johann Sebastian Bach, to write for and on them their immortal masterworks. The tone of the early clavichord was very thin, small and shortlived, but of singular purity and delicacy.

These characteristics the clavichord retained later, when the instrument grew in size and when several pedals were added to it. The tone grew to be louder, fuller, more amenable to shadings, but it still retained the peculiar lute-like quality of strings twanged by a quill of leather, metal, or other suitable material. Therefore he who would play on our modern pianos the compositions of Chambonnières (1600-1670), Daquin (1694-1772), François Couperin (1668-1733), Rameau (1683-1764), all French composers; Johann Adolf Hasse (1699-1783), Kuhnau (1660-1722), Carl Philipp Emanuel Bach (1714-1788), German composers; Francesco Durante (1684-1755), Padre Martini (1706-1784), Domenico Paradisi 1710-1792), Domenico Scarlatti 1685-1757), Italian composers: Orlando Gibbons (1583-1625), Byrd (1543-1623), Tallis (1515?-1585), Bull (1563-1628), English composers; Antonio de Cabezon (1510-1566), Spanish composer (to cite only these names among others) -- he, I say, who would play their compositions in a fulminative, massive, orchestral manner, resulting, on our modern pianos, in a formidable *fortissimo*, would commit an obviously gross breach of style. A moderate *forte*, at times only *mf*, should be the tonal limit.

The staccatos should be fine, dainty; the technic deft, agile and of pearly quality; the accentuation should be neat, precise and firm, but not vigorous in our modern sense. The lively tempos should be played somewhat less rapidly than we conceive them nowadays. The *Allegro* was not then quite so rapid as our modern *Allegro*, yet it had all the requisite liveliness of motion, (See the chapter on "Agogics" Book VI).

Regarding the further agogic treatment of those old compositions it would, of course, be a gross mistake of style to play them with the *tempo rubato* with which Chopin's works may be invested. A strict adherence to the time, a rhythm kept up without irregularities, these are necessary when playing the old masters, which does not mean of course that different subjects and contrasting periods should not each have a slightly different tempo.

All grace notes should be executed correctly, in accordance with the then prevailing custom. (See the chapter on "Embellishments").

The pedal should be used very sparingly, but its skillful employment is allowable. (See the chapter on "The Artistic Employment of the Piano Pedals" Book VI).

Johann Sebastian Bach

We are confronted with a different task when interpreting the piano compositions of Johann Sebastian Bach whose mighty mind conceived and wrought ahead of his time. Such genius as his survives tastes and fashions.

The piano compositions of Bach give an impression of such perfectly achieved unity, cohesion of ideas and unconstrained development of the thematic material that one is not aware of the restricted tonal range that lay at Bach's command. He usually writes between  and  In the forty-eight Preludes and Fugues of the "Well-Tempered Clavichord" the note  appears only three times; it is the lowest note in the Well-Tempered Clavichord. It is almost superfluous to say that this is due to the limited resources of the instruments of that period. This consideration justifies in some cases the "doubling" of bass notes, that is to say, the playing in octaves of the single notes written by Bach.

Fugue in C Minor, Book I

Fugue in D Major, Book I

From a dynamic standpoint we should remember that Bach never wrote *ppp* nor *fff*, not even *ff*. (See the chapter on "The Artistic Employment of Dynamics", Book VI). Such extremes of dynamic force, or of softness, easily obtainable on modern pianos were not dreamed of then.

An exception may be made for the mighty "Chromatic Fantasy and Fugue", the proportions of which are so broad that they justify a commensurate dynamic treatment, especially if played in a large concert hall.

Considered agogically, Bach's compositions must be played in strict time, without agogic nuances and without *rubato*. But the lively tempos may be played much more rapidly than those of the early clavichordists. Bach could play rapidly! (See the chapter on "Agogics", Book VI).

The correct execution of all trills and ornaments, (see the chapter on "Embellishments in Music") is one of the important factors for playing in their true style the compositions of the older classics. I might cite, as an obvious example, that to execute a trill with alternating hands when playing the piano compositions of Bach would be a flagrant breach of style.

Johann Sebastian Bach was the first great composer to use the thumb on the black keys, not occasionally, but as often as needed. This epoch-making innovation necessarily brought with it a less stilted, less rigid manner of playing the piano. Yet Bach's mode of playing was reposeful and quiet. The testimony of contemporary musicians convinces one of the broad, majestic and impressive manner in which the great Bach is said to have played. Full chords abound in his works, but the frail structure of the clavichords and clavicembalos of his time precluded any too great massiveness or forcefulness of execution. Double notes, meant as such, and not as part of the ever prevalent polyphonic style, occur seldom; scales in thirds and in sixths, never. Hence the scales in thirds and in sixths added by Hans von Bülow in his edition of Bach's Chromatic Fantasy and Fugue are a breach of style and should never be played; indeed, few, if any, of the great piano virtuosos use them.

Chromatic Fantasy and Fugue
JOHANN SEBASTIAN BACH

Prelude in B♭ Major (Book I)

JOHANN SEBASTIAN BACH

No virtuosity in octaves is required; everything is finger-work, but of the highest order and nearly always polyphonic. The eminent French pedagogue and theorist, F. Le Couppey, once wrote: "An artist whose refined taste equaled his erudition - Amédée Méreaux - says most excellently, 'The legato playing is best suited for the execution of the works of Johann Sebastian Bach. The hands should not make any unnecessary movement, nor lose their natural position, even in the most rapid passages!'"

The employment of the damper pedal is absolutely warranted when playing Bach's compositions, especially those that, by their context, tempo and general character, make demands which could hardly be met in those days, owing to the limited means of the instruments then used, but which can be satisfied fully on our modern pianos. (See the chapter, "The Artistic Employment of the Piano Pedals," Book VI.)

The suggestions and advice given should enable the earnest, truth-seeking pianist to do justice to Bach's compositions as they were played in his time. Yet, far be it from me to intimate that the resources of our modern, magnificent pianos should not be used when playing his works. That which would be a serious fault of style in playing Rameau (contemporary of Bach) is not serious, or even a fault, when the piano works of the great German are considered. His genius transcended time and means. The proof of this is that none of his piano works loses in plasticity of form, nor texture, values and perspective, to use the painter's vocabulary, when performed with all the resources that our pianos offer.

Georg Friederich Händel

What has been said of the compositions of Bach applies also, although in a slightly different degree, to those of Händel.

The two great Germans show marked affinity in their broad, polyphonic and virtuoso employment of the piano — more properly speaking, of the clavichord and clavicembalo. This is especially noticeable in Händel's magnificent Suites for piano, which nowadays are most unjustly neglected by the majority of pianists. We find there, as in the compositions of Bach, a wealth of melodic ideas, the same mastery of counterpoint and fugue, the same loftiness of ideals and breadth of execution. Witness the Suite No. 3, in D minor. What boldness of design and of execution! What virtuosity exacted in the Prelude!

The theme of the fugue is energetic, rhythmic, inspiring! In the Augener edition a modern version of the Suites is often appended to the original; it makes for greater power, yet does not violate the style of the composition.

Jean-Philippe Rameau – Domenico Scarlatti

They were born only two years apart (Rameau in 1683; Scarlatti in 1685), yet what a difference in their mode of musical expression! The affected, stilted ornaments which are ever prevalent in the works of Rameau and of Couperin seldom, if ever, appear in the piano compositions of Scarlatti. Rameau has been credited with being the founder of our harmonic system, while some historians trace to Scarlatti the paternity of modern piano virtuosity. In its showy, glittering sense this distinction is not entirely misplaced. Although the crossing of hands in piano playing was used by Bach (see as an example among others, the *Gigue* (last movement) of the Partita in B flat major,) it remained for Scarlatti to exploit this device to the full, in a virtuoso manner. Some of his sonatas (they are all in one movement) remain to this day a test for accuracy and virtuoso daring.

Sonata in A Major
DOMENICO SCARLATTI

Franz Joseph Haydn

Haydn and Mozart were contemporaries. Under the influence of their genius music suddenly developed in directions hitherto unknown.

Haydn, whom we now call the Father of the Symphony, gave to the orchestra, a role, an importance, not dreamed of before. In similar manner his piano sonatas are to be considered as the prototype of the modern sonata. They are so melodious, so fresh in invention and clever in workmanship, that there is no valid reason for their disappearance from the concert programs. Their style breathes at times simplicity and joyousness, at others a manly, vigorous spirit.

Sonata in E♭ Major (Cotta edition No.17)

JOSEPH HAYDN

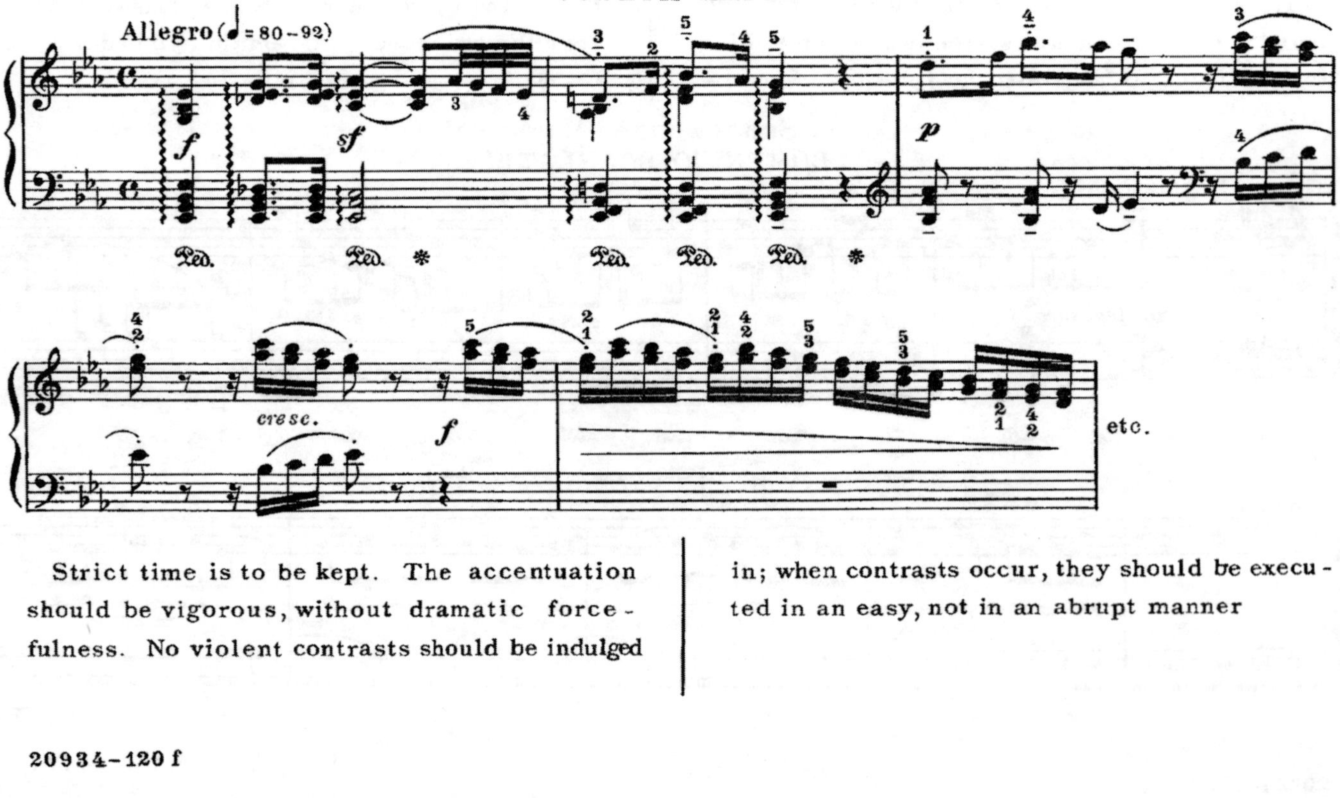

Strict time is to be kept. The accentuation should be vigorous, without dramatic forcefulness. No violent contrasts should be indulged in; when contrasts occur, they should be executed in an easy, not in an abrupt manner

Sonata in A♭ Major (Cotta edition No.16)

JOSEPH HAYDN

Wolfgang Amadeus Mozart

Jahn, the authoritative biographer, says of Mozart's manner of playing the piano: "He insisted mainly that the player should have a 'quiet, steady hand,' the natural ease, flexibility, and smooth rapidity of which should be so cultivated that the passages would 'flow like oil'; he did not counsel the practice of *tours de force* (extraordinary feats) which might be prejudicial to these qualities. His first requirements were the delivery of 'every note, turn, etc., correctly and decidedly, and with appropriate expression and taste.' He cautions players against over-rapidity of execution, not only of passages which are strictly connected, but also of those where liberties against strict time seem more allowable. He was strongly opposed to violations of time. 'It is much easier to play fast than to play slowly,' he remarks. 'Many notes may be dropped from passages, and none will notice it, but is it beautiful? The right hand may play faster than the left, and none will perceive it, but is it beautiful?'

"He placed correctness at the head of the list of qualities essential to first-rate playing and added to it ease and certainty in the execution of unusual technical difficulties, delicacy and good taste in delivery, and, above all, that power of breathing life and emotion into the music and of so expressing its meaning as to place the performer for the moment on a level with the creator of the work before him. We must be content to accept the enthusiastic testimony of the public, of connoisseurs and of accomplished fellow-artists, who all agree that Mozart indisputably ranked highest among virtuosi, by virtue of his fulfilment of all these conditions. When we find Clementi declaring that he never heard anyone play so intellectually and gracefully as Mozart, Dittersdorf finding art and fine taste united in his playing, and Haydn asserting with tears in his eyes that he could never forget Mozart's interpretation, because it 'reached the heart,' the simple expressions of such men are more eloquent than the most emphatic hyperbole."

It is evident that only a quiet "deportment" and a simple, not forceful, finger action, productive of the so-called "pearly touch," will obtain these results. Noteworthy is Mozart's sarcasm directed to pianists who "play so fast that one cannot distinguish clearly what they do." A virtuoso octave technic is not needed for the piano works of Mozart; neither massive -

ness nor orchestral color in chord- playing. Consequently, it is a mistake, when playing the so-called "Turkish March" from his lovely A minor Sonata (Mozart designated it "Alla Turca") to try to emulate the sonority of a military band.

(All editions urge, in a specially written foot-note, that the grace-notes should be played on the beat, that is to say that the first of the three grace-notes should be played at the same time than the octave in the right hand. The reasons why this is *wrong*, and in fact *impossible* to do without destroying absolutely the rhythm, are given in the Chapter "Embellishments", Book VII.)

Ludwig van Beethoven

When we think of him we involuntarily pause and, metaphorically speaking, take off our hats. Here we are on the threshold of a new art. Pearliness of touch! Passages that flow like oil! Who can think of them now! The man discarded the powdered wig of Haydn and of Mozart. It was his own jet black, shaggy hair that shook in the glow and passion of his powerful playing.

Seer and prophet, he brings to mind the rugged, immense "Thinker" of Michelangelo and of Rodin. He has sung the joys and sorrows of mankind with such depth and strength of conception and of expression as to place the masterworks which he has left us forever out of the reach of the tides of whims, fads and fashions. They will endure while man lives, for they are the vibrant expression of his better, nobler self.

"The greatest composer of all times"-such has been, for a century, the verdict of all enlightened, true musicians of all schools and climes. None has equaled him in epic strength, depth, breadth and height, and that is the reason why those too young, too weak or too shallow do not understand him and often do not like him.

Conceived by a mighty mind, depicting the entire range of human emotions, with the orchestra ever present in its wealth of color and disregarding technical difficulties entirely, the piano works of Beethoven compelled a new manner of playing that instrument. Virile, rugged strength, allied to feminine (not effeminate) grace; strong, yet supple fingers, wrists and arms, great forcefulness of accent and delicacy of touch -- all these are needed when playing Beethoven. But more than that, one must have lived -- for the canvas on which he wields his mighty brush is so large that eyes too young cannot understand its heroic proportions.

Here we are freed from any considerations as to the instrument for which Beethoven wrote. Every piano composition up to Op. 106 was written for the clavicembalo, or harpsichord; from Op. 106 on for the "hammer-klavier" and that on which we play nowadays. What I said about Bach applies, only oh! so much more, to Beethoven. He wrote ahead of time -- for all times. He wrote, not for the string-twanged clavicembalo nor for the string-struck pianos, he wrote on our hearts, for our souls. All the emotions that sway mankind, all the thoughts that have transformed races, the aspirations and the faith, precursors of great deeds, dreams, legends, the metaphysical contemplations of great minds that tower above common mankind like the cloud-hidden peaks of the Himalayas, the quiet singing and praying of the mother rocking a cradle -- all are but the strings of the huge instrument for which Beethoven wrote.

From a dynamic standpoint, one of the salient characteristics of the style of Beethoven is the frequent recurrence of contrast. These contrasts should be executed as intended, with sudden transitions from *forte* to *piano*, and vice versa, and not by melting one shading into another. (See the chapter on "The Artistic Employment of Dynamics", Book VI.)

Regarding the tempo we are absolutely free to employ any legitimate agogic means that will help us to faithfully reproduce the great composer's intentions. Czerny has left it on record that Beethoven, when playing his own compositions, at times accelerated his tempos. This vehemence is, of course, to be indulged in, and encouraged in others, only where the needs of a fiery declamation justify it. Coupled with this breadth and fire of execution are required great energy and forcefulness of accentuation.

Ries, one of the very few pupils of Beethoven, says in his "Notizen" (page 106) alluding to the *Sonate Pathétique:* "In general he (Beethoven) played his compositions in a very moody manner; he nevertheless kept strictly accurate time, occasionally, but very seldom, accelerating the tempi. On the other hand, in the performance of a crescendo passage, he would make the time ritardando, which produced a beautiful and highly striking effect".

Anton Schindler was not only one of the most intimate friends of Beethoven and his almost constant companion for many years, but a musician of sensibility, culture and discernment. What he has to say in regard to the style of playing of Beethoven and to the characteristics of his piano compositions is therefore of considerable interest. He writes: "Now, with regard to the sonatas, I have further to observe that the hints which I received from Beethoven on the subject of their composition and the proper style of their performance, had direct reference to only a few of these compositions. Still, no doubt, many persons will be gratified by what I have to communicate. To the intelligent lover of music, these hints will afford matter for reflection, whereby he may not only more thoroughly comprehend the works in question, but also, by the help of the key thus obtained, open for himself a path to the knowledge of other compositions of the like kind, imbued with the like soul and spirit.... In short, all music performed by his hands appeared to undergo a new creation. These wonderful effects were in a great degree produced by his uniform legato style, which was one of the most remarkable peculiarities of his playing.

"All the pieces which I have heard Beethoven himself play were, with few exceptions, given without any constraint as to the rate of time. He adopted a tempo rubato in the proper sense of the term, as subject and situation might demand, without the slightest approach to caricature. On the subject of accentuation I may state, as a general remark, that Beethoven gave prominent force to all appoggiaturas, particularly the minor second, even in running passages, and in slow movements his transition to the principal note was as delicately managed as it could have been by the voice of a singer."

Beethoven, like all great natures, could be (and often was) feminine; but he never was effeminate. His rugged nature emphasized both softness and strength. Moreover, he had constantly in his mind the orchestra as background. This alone will guide us in our desire and endeavor to be true to the Beethovenian style. It is for this reason of orchestral conception that his sonatas abound in passages that are 'unklaviermässig,' as the Germans say, which means "unpianistic."

How much easier would be

Sonata Op.57

LUDWIG van BEETHOVEN

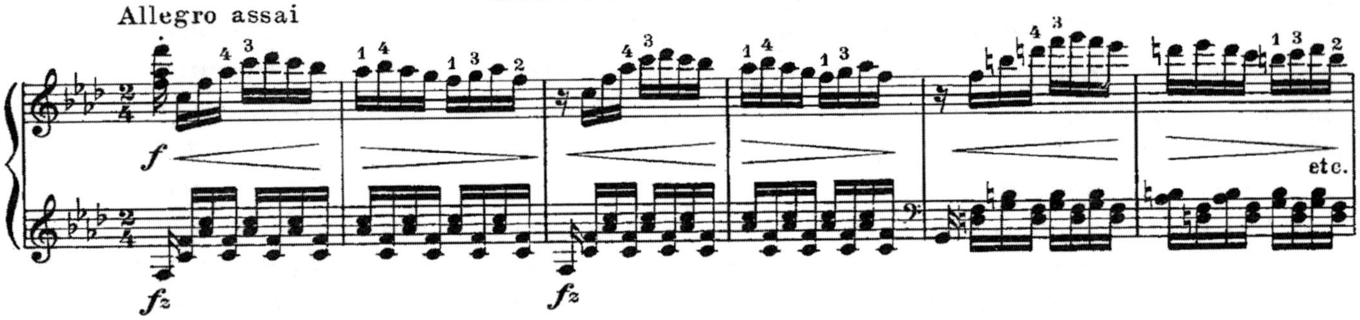

than what Beethoven wrote:

yet in this case any "facilitation" is inadmissible if we would be true to Beethoven's intentions, and not violate his style of writing. The above given facilitation provides nothing but the impression of a sort of tremolo, which brings into melodic prominence and gives rhythmic weight to the two major thirds; A flat-C and G-B, whereas in Beethoven's version we hear the horns sounding:

the first and second violins playing:

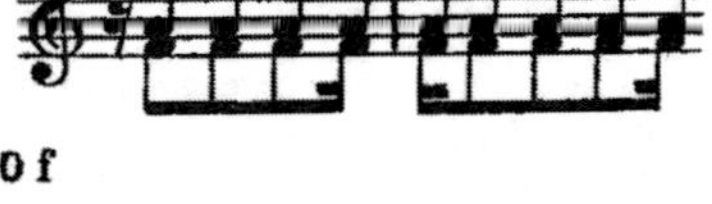

And this is answered by the trombones:

and by the violas and 'cellos, playing with short up and down bow strokes:

This is one of the additional reasons why it is difficult to understand and to play Beethoven well. It is necessary to have a knowledge of the orchestral instruments, of their tone color and of the way in which they are used.

Carl Maria von Weber

The name of Carl Maria von Weber has well-nigh disappeared from our programs. Yet what elegance of writing, what verve and boisterousness of expression, what scintillating technic are contained in his works! Fleet, agile and strong fingers are needed when playing the C major Sonata with its last, brilliant, well-known "Perpetual Movement."

There is a well defined chivalric spirit in his compositions. They are joyous, vigorous, seldom sentimental. The technical demands are quite high but of a healthy nature. The technic of octaves assumes suddenly a startling significance and brilliance. Passages in octaves like these:

Konzertstück

(for piano and orchestra)

CARL MARIA von WEBER

were not even dreamed of before Weber's time and it may be safely asserted that he was the first to develop the technic of octaves in a modern virtuoso sense. The general characteristics of his style require strict time and firm rhythm, which are nevertheless allied to elegance of execution.

Franz Schubert

What lovely memories his name alone evokes! Only he who can understand and appreciate the freshness, the child-like, open-hearted loveliness of his nature will portray him faithfully.

He sang. In poverty, through tribulations,

through his short life he sang, and some of his songs will be on the lips of dying mankind.

This singing quality of his music is portrayed in his lengthy but admirable sonatas; in his "Moments Musicaux," gems of ineffable beauty; in his vivacious "Impromptus"; in his great "Wanderer" Fantasy. The considerable additions and amplifications made by Liszt in his edition of the "Wanderer" Fantasy preserve the spirit of this great composition and in no way violate its style.

The demands made on the pianist's technic are high. The dynamic treatment is full-blooded, highly dramatic at times. Agogically, the same considerations as when playing Beethoven prevail; no Chopin-like rubato, but great elasticity of tempo. The declamation of his melodic context should be more "vocal" than instrumental, but not always so.

Fantasy Op. 15

(Wanderer - Fantasy)
in the Liszt edition

FRANZ SCHUBERT

Der Wanderer

Adagio

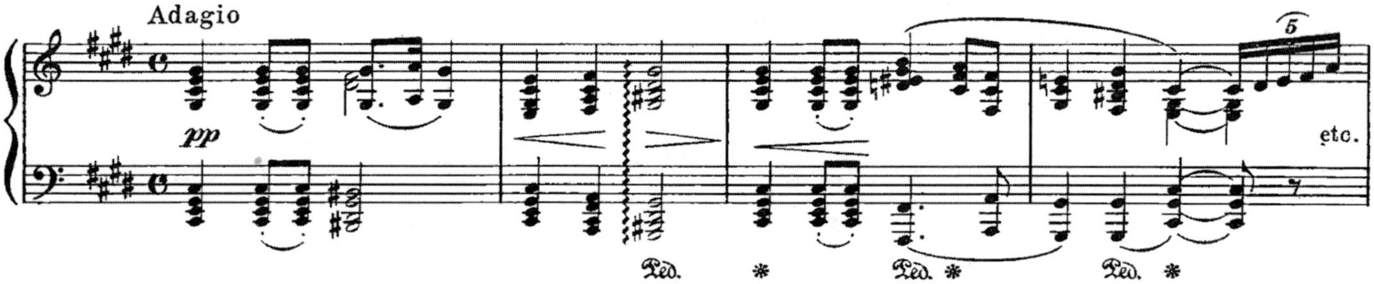

"In my opinion this movement should be played very slowly and pathetically - *ab imo pectore*" (Franz Liszt).

To play Schubert is to place oneself in communion with one of the most spontaneous, melodious and lovable poets in music.

Felix Mendelssohn - Bartholdy

In America it is the affectation of many an amateur, and also of many a professional musician, to sneer at the mention of his name, just as some overgrown boys and girls, and likewise nevergrown men and women, are apt to sneer at the novels of Charles Dickens. "Old-fashioned, passé, out of style," these are some of the mildest expessions they use. They are only to be pitied, those whose impressions in art and in literature were so feeble during their childhood and youth that they cannot recall them all their lives. And blessed are those whose youth remains perennial, because the intensity and vividness of their impressions are never lessened, and they are faithful and grateful, ever, to the master minds that once thrilled them with joy and happiness.

In order to play Mendelssohn well you must have melody in your heart. In many of his songs without words, the influence of the endearing, intensely poetic German folk-songs is noticeable. A tinge of very slight melancholy, of *Heimweh*, at times suffuses his works. A good legato in the delivery of the cantilena is needed here. The dynamic treatment is, of course, complete from ***ppp*** to ***fff***. The agogic treatment becomes freer, for Mendelssohn belongs to the so-called Romantic Period. To play his works with the forcefulness, nay the gruffness, which at times is required in Beethoven, would be an error of judgment, a mistake of style. Mendelssohn is well-bred, elegant, yet he is also virile. His "Variations Sérieuses" are essentially strong-fibred, despite the melancholy and softness of the theme.

So are also his splended, broadly conceived Preludes and Fugues, foremost among which stands the Prelude and Fugue in E minor Op.35. So are also both his concertos in G minor and D minor, his Fantasy in F♯ minor.

Frederick Chopin -- Robert Schumann

Instinctively we couple their names. They were born in the same year, 1810, and the marvelous tone-poems which they have left us were created approximately during the same period of time.

Chopin is the only great composer who devoted himself entirely to the piano. He wrote nothing for the orchestra alone, nor for chamber music, if we except his trio for piano, violin and 'cello. Therefore, there are some who would deny him a place on Olympus next to Bach, Mozart, Beethoven. But greatness is not to be judged, by the variety of means of expression used, but by the wide range and the strength and vividness of the emotions depicted. We do not rank Aristophanes beneath Sophocles because the first wrote only satires and comedies and the second only tragedies and dramas; nor do we deny the greatness of Homer because he wrote neither dramas nor tragedies nor comedies nor satires, but *only* the "Iliad" and the "Odyssey."

The piano was the medium that Chopin chose, and for it he wrote some of the most perfect tone-creations that enrich humanity. His power of expression is amazing. By turns lyrical, dramatic, pathetic, heroic, epic, Chopin has appealed to and searched into our inmost hearts as few, if any, have done since him. It is a poor tribute to his mémory to say, as some have said, that he was a mediocre musician, knew no counterpoint, and that only in a couple of places, in his entire works, is there anything like an "imitation." This assertation is utterly unfounded. The following skillfully executed canons clearly prove it:

Mazurka in C Major, Op. 56, No. 2
FREDERICK CHOPIN

Mazurka Op. 50, No. 3
FREDERICK CHOPIN

What matters it if Chopin never wrote a fugue! He has sung, in vibrant, imperishable accents that which, dormant or awake, lives in every human heart.

Beethoven wrote vast problems and struggles of mankind against fate and his joys and sorrows are so big that they belong to the entire human race and therefore we, single individuals, sometimes fail to understand him. Chopin wrote for the heart of man and woman. All that can gladden or pain he wrote and in what appealing accents!

In his works, and they are nearly all for the piano, we live our lives again. Not one string of our heart does he leave untouched.

With the Chopin waltzes is coupled the gilded vision of aristocratic Parisian salons, dainty perfumes, beautiful women and courtly knights. With the nocturnes is evoked a pale, melancholy Chopin, at whose feet sit marquises and princesses, who lift their adoring eyes toward the heaven-inspired poet-musician. For this fanciful picture Turgenieff is much to blame. The Chopin waltzes are indeed "distinguished" in the extreme, and there can be no question but that he raised this form of dance to the high level of a poetic musical creation: (See the Chapter, "Conception-Interpretation"). Also in his nocturnes has Chopin done more and better than others have done before or since. The nocturnes of Field, so unjustly neglected, are the prototype of this form of composition, and many of them are real gems of fresh, melodic musical inspiration. Yet how they pale into lustreless tints when brought into comparison with Chopin's nocturnes! In these, all the varying shades of tender or passionate yearnings, of melancholy retrospect, of the *Zal*--the unutterable pain and regret of all things--are glimpsed, mirrored or sung directly to us, in soft penetrating, strangely moving accents.

Not always thus. His soft, wooing tones, his velvet touch are delicacy, not weakness. When the flame flares up in his soul, a mighty grip of steel clutches our wrists, and it is a manly, heroic apparition that bids us follow him, as with outstretched arm, he points to the deeper, devastating tragedies of life.

Ballade in F Major, Op.38

FREDERICK CHOPIN

Presto con fuoco e molto agitato

You of the puny soul, of the dry little heart, you the weak-fibred, do not play the finale of the Nocturne in B major, op. 32! Do not attempt the tragic grandeur of his C minor Nocturne, of his two Etudes in A minor and both in C minor in which he hurls forth his passionate, throbbing protest against Poland's downfall! For here the greater, the real Chopin looms up, and you would fail, you would not understand!

No one has written nocturnes and waltzes of such fascinating, dazzling brilliancy, or so suffused with poetic charm or tragic pathos as those of the Polish master; and yet they embody only a little part of Chopin's genius. With them, through them alone, we would never know the mighty sweep and strength of him who, throwing aside the aquarelle brush gripped a chisel and carved huge blocks of granite and marble. Michelangelo and Botticelli united into one creative personality seem impossible; yet this was Chopin in his clearly marked duality.

None can exceed the heroic and martial valor of his great soul. In his *Polonaises* F sharp minor, A flat major, A major, C minor, reverberate the tramp of armies, the boom of cannons, the sinister howl of grim war. Chopin, the morbid dreamer of nocturnes, the elegant composer of aristocratic waltzes, we all know; but not all have as yet fathomed the might and sweep of his greater works; the Fantasy in F minor, the four Ballades, the four Scherzos, the great Polonaises, the Sonatas in B flat minor and in B minor, the Etudes and some of the Preludes and Mazurkas..... Our piano technic has had to grow because of him: scales in thirds, chromatic thirds, fourths, sixths, the boldest passages in octaves, arpeggios of superoctave range coursing through the entire keyboard, call for endurance and strength as never before.

To play Chopin well you must have imagination, fancy and depth of feeling. It would take a book by itself to write adequately about the wonderful versatility evidenced in his works.

We need now, when playing his compositions, a technic far more developed than when we play Mendelssohn, or even Beethoven. In fact, Chopin created a new technic. Flights like these:-

were unknown before him. The employment of stretches over an octave is frequent, yet the smallest hand can play them if they are practised intelligently. Thirds, fourths, sixths, abound, also bold passages in octaves. The dynamical treatment is complete. Agogically a new feature appears: the preponderance of the *tempo rubato*. Although employed before, yet only in Chopin does it find full application. Liszt has described it as the rays of sunlight passing through trembling leaves. It is difficult to describe in words how to play *rubato*. Perhaps this may give an idea; the right hand plays with full freedom and is unrestricted by the sense of time, while the left hand constantly and gently brings it back to the prescribed tempo.

The accentuation fluctuates between the softest and the fieriest imaginable. Trills may, in a few instances (not in many), be executed by both hands in alternation. The pedals are used freely.

To play his Nocturnes well does not imply that one can play his tremendous Ballades, Scherzos, Polonaises, his Etudes, Sonatas, Concertos.

Chopin is the poet of the piano, and it needs not only a poetic but also a virile nature to understand him and to play his works adequately.

Robert Schumann

Schumann's style is widely different. A more massive technic is required here, for he writes much and often in chords and in orchestra style.

To appreciate and do justice to his style of writing is not easy for those who do not fully fathom and feel the meaning of the German word "Gemüt" which means mood, state of the soul, poetic temperament, all rolled into one. Besides, some of his most notable compositions for piano are founded upon, or derived from, carnival scenes, and how can anyone explain to somebody who has not lived in countries in which the carnival is traditionally kept up, every year, with its symbolistic costumes of Columbine, Pierrot, Arlequin--how can he explain the spirit of it, the peculiarities inherent in and the difference between these carnival types that have come down to us from mediæval times! Therefore, he who would play understandingly the "Carnaval" the "Faschingschwank" Carnival Scenes, the "Papillons", must become conversant with the meaning and spirit of the carnival and carnival types. This will aid him in doing justice to the airy flight of fancy that breathes through these compositions.

Schumann's nature was essentially "schwärmerisch", a German word which, like the word "Gemüt", described before, has no direct equivalent in English, but which may loosely be described "dreamy", "yearning", "enamoured" and "rapt up in poetic ideals". Add to all this a fantasy which tinged all he wrote with a wealth of romantic feeling akin to that of the mediæval "Meistersängers" and you have the Schumann of the Fantasy Pieces Op. 12 and Op. 129, of the "Kinderscenen" (Childhood Scenes), of the Kreisleriana--the musical portraiture of The Tales of Hoffmann - of the "Intermezzos", and the great Fantasy Op. 17.

No cold, unimaginative nature can hope to play these bewitching compositions in a manner that will reveal their inner meaning and be true to their style.

Hidden or revealed, the two sides of his dual nature, "Eusebius" and "Florestan", are ever present in his compositions. He has himself described these two fanciful aspects of his nature both in prose and in music, and some of his remarkable articles in the "Neue Zeitschrift für Musik", founded by him, are signed with their names.

Both gave birth to the "Carnaval", that matchless collection of carnival scenes and carnival types, each a gem of joyous and exquisite workmanship; to the "Papillons", "Faschingschwank" (Carnival Scenes); to the "Davidsbündlertänze" (David-Leaguers Dances). Exuberance of an ever youthful, ardent spirit is manifest in them all. It is interesting to observe that in the first edition of the "Davidsbündlertänze" the eighteen numbers which it contains are, all of them, signed either F and E. (Florestan and Eusebius), or with only one of these initials. In the second edition of this work all these initials, as well as the poetical effusions written over numbers nine and eighteen have been taken out. This, however, does not obliterate the spirit in which this collection of little pieces was conceived.

Davidsbündlertänze

(David - Leaguers Dances)

ROBERT SCHUMANN

Hierauf schloss Florestan und es zuckte ihm schmerzlich um die Lippen.

Hereupon Florestan stopped, and a sad emotion was visible around his lips.

No. 9

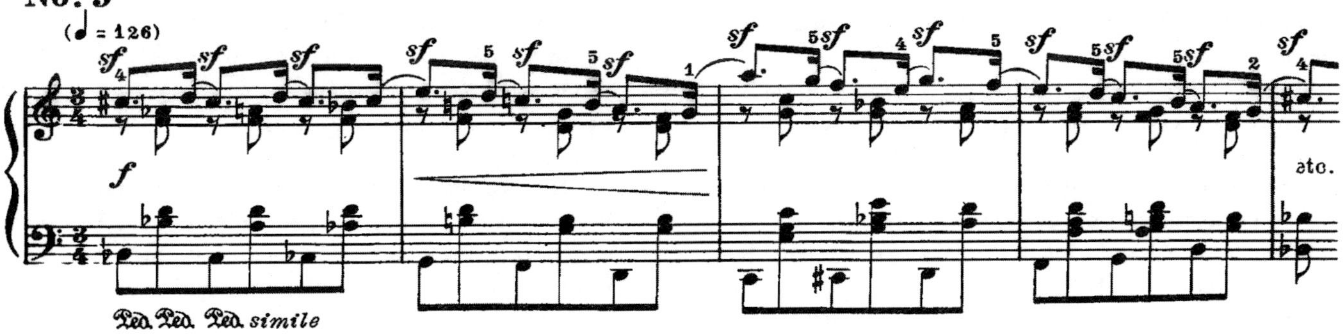

His "Novelettes," which title means "little novels" or "stories," bear the impress of the true romantic German nature, ever fond of the ballads, legends and fairy tales with which the literature abounds, while his technically very difficult "Etudes Symphoniques" are the product of an essentially strong, virile personality.

The Concerto in A minor is the concomitant of all the lovable traits in Schumann's nature. A wealth of invention and assertive manliness coupled to the most exquisite, tender grace, make of this work one of the greatest ever written for piano and orchestra.

Curiously enough, while Schumann's piano compositions often wear an orchestral garb, his symphonies give, at times, the impression of piano music transcribed for the orchestra.

In matters of dynamics, agogics and accentuation, what has been said of Chopin applies also to Schumann, with the added tinge of orchestral massiveness.

Will what has been said afford a clue how to do justice to the style of Schumann? I believe it will for some, I hope it may for the others.

Franz Liszt --Anton Rubinstein

Franz Liszt

If Chopin is the poet, Liszt is the virtuoso *par excellence* and both he (1811) and Anton Rubinstein (1829) will ever stand as the two highest exponents of piano playing. Anton Rubinstein at the piano was a lion; an onrushing whirlwind of fury and passion that no barriers of technical difficulties could stay; the breadth and sweep of his playing were appalling and thrilling, yet the lion's paw could caress the keys with a touch like velvet, and what a tone he drew from the piano! Liszt, on the other hand, was the magician evoking all the splendor of the East; its hot, surging voluptuousness, the dazzling brilliancy of gorgeously set gems But he could also let loose all the lightning and thunder of a torrential temperament, and his playing, in the palmy days of his virtuosity, is said to have exercised over his hearers the same witchery that was attributed to Paganini.

Saint-Saëns, himself one of the greatest of French pianists, whose piano compositions, especially the concertos, have enlarged not a little the brilliant and effective repertoire of the modern pianist, says in his "Portraits et Souvenirs":- "One would hardly believe with what radiance, what magic prestige the name of Liszt appeared to the young musicians during the early days of the Imperial period; a name so strange for us Frenchmen, sharp and cutting like a blade of steel, traversed by its slavic Z as if by the flash of lightning. As an artist and as a man he seemed to belong to the legendary world.

"The majority of the pieces which he had published seemed impossible of execution to anybody but him and they were so indeed when one considers the precepts of the old method which prescribed immobility, the elbows immovable, near the body, with a limited action left to the fingers and to the forearms . . . . . .
The influence of Liszt on the destiny of the piano has been immense, I see nothing to be compared to it except the revolution brought about by Victor Hugo in the mechanism of the French language. It is more powerful than the influence of Paganini in the world of the violin."

It is a significant fact that with the exception of Richard Wagner-- shall Hector Berlioz be mentioned in the same breath?--the world's greatest composers were pianists, not merely piano *players* but piano *virtuosos*. J. S. Bach, Händel, Rameau, Couperin, Domenico Scarlatti, Haydn, Mozart, Beethoven, Weber, Schubert, Chopin, Schumann, Mendelssohn, Brahms, Rubinstein, Saint-Saëns,-- all were accomplished performers whose pianistic skill kept pace with their creative powers. Yet it is first and foremost as composers that the world honors their names.

Not so with Franz Liszt. His musical heritage to us is priceless, notwithstanding what the dried-up, pedantic musicians may say. They may try to disparage the musical value of his Rhapsodies, Transcriptions and other virtuoso pieces; but how much poorer we would be if we had them not, these wondrous Rhapsodies, now tinged with the melancholy of the *Zal*, anon aglow with untamed passion and reckless energy. The Hungarian Rhapsodies of Liszt will stay with us as long as red blood courses through human veins.

And consider the dazzling brilliancy of his Transcriptions! Who can remain unmoved when he hears, well played, the unmatched Paraphrase of Verdi's "Rigoletto," the stupendous transcription of Wagner's "Tannhäuser" Overture, Mendelssohn's "Midsummer Night's Dream," Senta's Ballade from "The Flying Dutchman," and many others! As for his piano pieces, what a galaxy of master-works! His Sonata in B minor, his Sonata "Quasi Fantasia," his two-piano concertos, the Hungarian Fantasy, the Waldesrauschen, Gnomenreigen, Liebesträume, Consolations. the Ballades in D flat major and in B minor, the Polonaise in E major, his Concert Etudes, Paganini-Etudes, his "Années de Pélerinage"-- a score of gems-- his "Funérailles," one of the three greatest funeral marches ever written, (the other two being by Beethoven and by Chopin). And this enumeration of his most effective piano pieces is by no means complete.

Liszt is the creator of the Symphonic Poem for orchestra. "Les Préludes" form part of the standard repertoire for every orchestra in the world. He also wrote magnificent oratorios.

Yet it is Liszt, the pianist, who looms up, gigantic, on the horizon of history, and we think of him, not as the creator of scores of masterworks--enough to insure fame for a half- dozen composers-- but as the hero of piano playing.

What Orpheus is in Mythology, what the wizard, demoniacal Paganini was for the violin, Liszt was, is, and perhaps will ever be, for the piano.

What are the essentials for a good, correct or superlatively brilliant rendition of Liszt's piano works? The technic must first of all be brilliant; that is to say, the pianist must have fingers strong enough to give a forceful articulation to the most rapid runs and arpeggios. The demands made on the technic are of the very highest. Liszt, like Chopin, revolutionized technic, and especially the *manner of playing*. The word "freedom" epitomizes best the character of his style. Every device of dynamics and agogics is called into play. Rubato, forcefulness, strict time, elastic time, lightness, massiveness, organ-like adaptations; they are all to be employed.

The alternate use of the hands in the execution of trills, scales, thirds, fourths, sixths and octaves reaches with Liszt a height of technical usefulness, brilliancy and display scarcely found elsewhere.

The scholastic player seldom does justice to the compositions of Liszt. Temperament, fire, passion, imagination, courage, daring-- all are needed here.

The sweeping brilliancy required in the reproduction of Liszt's Rhapsodies is to be expected only from mature players, from real virtuosos. Students, however, may feel and they often do, the surge, the tremendous sweep of Liszt's music which they have not the technical resources to express. It remains then for the teacher to lead them to a sufficient technical development.

Anton Rubinstein

Although Anton Rubinstein was one of the two greatest piano virtuosos the world has ever known, yet as a composer he has not brought great innovations and amplifications. But he has written for the piano so many works that form part of the standard, classic repertoire of the pianist that a short description of their style seems necessary.

Rubinstein had an enormous tone, by which is not meant strength when hitting the keys *ff*, but the natural volume and intensity of tone when playing a simple melody. He was fond of displaying this gift (which he cultivated through assiduous practice) and this should be kept in mind when we play his "Melodie" in F major, his Romance in E♭, the Barcarolles, the second movement of his Concerto in D minor.

Besides fullness of tone in "singing-quality" his style requires marked fire, I am tempted to say fierceness, of expression. Rubinstein, despite his strongly marked cosmopolitanism, (he humorously complained at times that the Russians considered him a German, and the Germans called him a Russian) was essentially a Russian, and often in his music flares up the wild impetuosity that characterizes the Slavic race. Witness his Concerto in D minor, his Lesghinka, Trot de Cavalerie, and many other compositions. His lovely Barcarolles show well the romantic, tender side of his nature.

Johannes Brahms

In the piano works of Johannes Brahms there looms up a technic for which Czerny's Exercises and Chopin's Etudes are no sufficient preparation. His music is at times massive, like Schumann's, but laid out on a far broader basis. He often uses arpeggios and technical designs exceeding the stretch of an octave, but unlike Chopin's they are "orchestral", not simply pianistic.

His Variations on a theme of Händel, and especially his two books of Variations on a theme of Paganini require a titanic technic, and consummate musicianship.

Brahms' music, like Schumann's reposes on German *Gemüt* and his melodies also have a folklore character. He certainly is more robust, at times gruffer, less tractable, than Schumann. Brahms, while essentially Germanic, discloses often in his music a deftness and versatility which may be traceable to the direct influence of Chopin and Liszt.

To play the compositions of Brahms well, breadth, strength and virility are needed and great tenderness also. To play his works with an exaggerated tempo rubato or with the sweet sentimentality consistent with a nocturne by Field would be as glaring an error of style as to execute a trill of Rameau with alternating hands. Yet Brahms can sing with sweetness and softness. His "Wiegenlied", his Capriccio in B minor are eloquent specimens. The real Brahms, however, is the Brahms of the Sonata Op.5, of the Intermezzos, of the three Rhapsodies, of the Ballades, of the Variations mentioned before. To do them justice is to be not only an accomplished technician, but a good musician as well.

Camille Saint-Saëns

Camille Saint-Saëns was one of the foremost composers, as well as pianists, that France has produced. To give a list of names of the great musicians who have written for the piano without mentioning Saint-Saëns, who has done so much for spreading, both through the pen and through his own playing, the admirable qualities of the French school, would be to leave that list incomplete.

Saint-Saëns was indeed a worthy representative of a school that has ever stood for purity in writing and in playing. His style is never dramatic, but singularly elegant and evidences the consummate musicianship that characterizes all he has written.

His Concertos will always form part of the classical repertoire, especially those in C minor and in G minor.

A highly cultivated technic is needed to play them, fleet fingers, light, rapid wrists, deft staccatos, fulminating octaves and above all, elegance of style.

The agogic treatment must be very strict. I have often heard him play and conduct the orchestra in private rehearsals; his adherence to an absolutely strict tempo, throughout an entire composition (even in such a fanciful work as his "Danse Macabre") was surprising and at times disconcerting. There is however, considerable latitude in this respect in pieces like his "Etude en Forme de Valse" (Etude in the Form of a Waltz.)

Edvard Grieg

Not to give him special mention in a chapter devoted to the study of style would be a flagrant injustice to a composer whose melodic, rhythmic and harmonic originality has influenced other composers and, unknown to them-- for Grieg is not the founder of a "School" and has no "followers"-- has paved the way for the more acceptable dissonances and harmonic combinations of the so-called modern school.

This originality and wide-spread influence are, I feel certain, acknowledged by all broadminded musicians.

Curiously enough the output of Grieg is not such as to form an integrant, neverfading part of the pianist's repertoire. Excepting his piano concerto, which has become a "classic", and his wondrously beautiful Ballade, his other piano compositions have been slowly receding from the concert-stage, where they once held sway, along with many a delightful but unjustly forgotten composition by Raff, Moszkowski, Godard and Chaminade, which have now reached the lower level of "drawing-room" pieces. Yet Grieg's "To Spring", his "Humoresques", "Holberg" Suite, and a score of lovely fantasy pieces deserved a better fate.

His three sonatas for piano and violin will ever be acknowledged among the most fragrant and most grateful examples of that beautiful realm of music which no pianist should neglect-- chamber music.

Grieg's Concerto and the Ballade require a virtuoso technic, for the demands made are of the highest order. Brilliancy and dash, an incisive rhythm, a romantic spirit are needed when interpreting his compositions; also an understanding of, and sympathy for, that strange blending of melancholy and reckless energy that typifies the temperament of Slavic, Finnish and Scandinavian races.

Claude Debussy

Debussy is the acknowledged founder and leader of the self-styled "modern" school, which appellation is in every way a misnomer.

His piano compositions and those of his followers, Ravel, Stravinsky, Schönberg, to mention only a few, aim at tone-color, description, "atmosphere", mood-delineation, but not at an emotional or intellectual development of musical ideas. The whole-tone scale, the succession of augmented fifths and fourths, and other characteristics of this school are all conducive to the formation of tone-color and of "atmosphere". This is the reason why, in order to play such compositions well and with the appropriate style, the musicianly education, intelligence and knowledge, the depth of feeling and the catholicity of taste necessary to perform beautifully the larger compositions of Bach, Beethoven, Schubert, Mozart, Chopin and Schumann, are not needed. This is the reason, too, why so many mediocre pianists and mediocre musicians, and likewise those who, having the talent, are too lazy and indolent to continue developing their latent musical powers, wave this banner of so called modernism to the *exclusion of any other*.

Not so with the vigorous, full-blooded and broadminded musician who has fed his soul, heart and intelligence on what the great masters in music have bequeathed him. He will readily accept anything "new" or "modern"--how quickly the new date fades into the past!-- provided that it ravishes his musical ear, touches his heart, fires his imagination or appeals to his intellect. Such compositions are eagerly welcomed, whether old or new.

But of how many such compositions can the "modernist" boast. His best output consists of a comparatively small number of colorful, pleasing pieces of small caliber; these deserve a place on the programs of the most serious minded musician. But to attempt to magnify them into masterworks destined to replace the classics - what folly!

In several of his compositions for piano Debussy displays an originality and a deftness of pastel-like coloring not evidenced by his many imitators. A good command over *pianissimo* and ***ppp***-- and be it observed again that most pianists neglect the acquisition of a sustained, true pianissimo-- is necessary when playing his piano compositions; also a clever use of the pedals. As examples may be cited, "La Cathédrale Engloutie", "Clair de Lune", "Danse" "La Soirée dans Grenade" and "Pour le Piano".

A resilient, light touch, a good employment of *rubato*, coupled with a keen sense of rhythm, an understanding of, and affinity for, what is vague, dreamy, whimsical and fantastic, a very generous but clever mode of employing the pedals-- these are the main requisites for playing, in their own style, the piano compositions of Debussy.

* * * * * *

Many a reader may be surprised at the omission in the preceding nomenclature, of the names of several eminent composers who have written extensively and beautifully for the piano, Raff, Tschaikowsky (whose piano concertos in B♭ minor and in G major form part of every piano virtuoso's repertoire) Arensky, Rachmaninoff, Paderewski, Moszkowski, Albeniz and other splendid composers; they all have contributed to enrich the repertoire of the pianist. Because of their genius we are better and happier. Nevertheless I have had to limit myself to the study of those composers whose eminence is so great that they have put the stamp of their individuality on the epoch in which they created their works.

Successful Playing

in

Public

Successful Playing In Public.

Suggestions and Advice ★★★★ Temperament and Fire — Restraint and Deliberation ★★★★ Boldness, Dash and Abandon — Prudence ★★★★ Daring — Carefulness, Preparation of keys ★★★★ Freedom of attitude and deportment, tempered by repose and poise ★★★★ Fear, Uncertainty — Authority Courage ★★★★ Blurred memory — Clear mental vision ★★★★ Absentmindedness — Mental concentration ★★★★ Nervousness — Complete command of self.

and

An Essay on "The Problem of Success in Public" by

LEOPOLD SCHMIDT

It would seem, after years of toil and devotion to his art, when a pianist has acquired a highly developed technic, a beautiful touch and tone, good rhythm, good command over dynamics and agogics, musical conception, interpretation, execution and rendition, that all he has to do is to step on the concert stage in order to win the brilliant success that is his due. Very often, however, this is not so, and many a deserving artist has failed in public -- even abandoned concert playing altogether -- because of his, or his teacher's, inability to understand the wide difference that exists between playing for oneself, or for a small number of friends and playing in public.

The mental attitude of a performer facing the public is a vital factor in the final gaining of success.

How shall he learn to so conduct himself that it will make no difference whether he is playing alone, or for a large audience?

Some persons are to the manner born. From the very first they feel at home when playing for others, whether in a room or on the stage; their minds remain as lucid and their nerves as quiet as when they play without auditors.

These beings are blessed by nature with the faculty of being oblivious to their surroundings. Let me add that they are to be considered as exceptions.

Tranquillity and a natural, free attitude -- in short, the absence of all nervousness when playing for people -- are, as a rule, the possessions of those who appeared in public when very young. This is the reason why all so-called wonder-children are absolutely free from stage fright when they reach the age at which they may command attention as artists rather than as prodigies.

What is stage fright?

In its acute form, it is mental and physical agony, an ordeal which makes public playing something to be dreaded and which, once gone through, is never forgotten. Even in its mild form it robs the player of full possession of his means. Can stage fright be overcome and dispelled forever? Yes.

The conditions for playing in public with ease and assurance are, first and foremost, complete confidence in one's own accuracy and a memory as infallible as is consistent with human frailty. And in addition, the performer must be secure in the knowledge that *music lives in his heart;* that his manner of playing has received the approval of an absolutely competent piano virtuoso who knows the effects and the perspective of the stage. Let us examine these points more closely.

Most performers do not realize what it is that they fear when appearing in public. If they would analyze their sensations and misgivings they would find that the reasons for their anxiety are the following:

More than anything else they are afraid of forgetting.

This has already been pointed out in the chapter on "The Art of Memorizing" and suggestions and advice have been given therein for making the memory clear, strong and faithful *in performance* as well as in practice. The necessity of having, on every page, one or two "memory goals" has been demonstrated. Finally, advice has been given on what to do if, in spite of perfect training, a slip occurs in public performance.

A careful consideration of that chapter will make a performer confident that as far as his memory is concerned he has nothing to fear.

Next to forgetting, a performer dreads most that he will strike wrong notes.

This subject has been treated exhaustively in the chapter on "Accuracy-- How to Play Without Striking Wrong Notes." Necessary suggestions, advice, and exercises have been given therein in order to insure absolutely accurate playing. That chapter should be read and *practised* carefully by every thoughtful student.

The most accurate performer, the greatest artist, cannot truthfully say, "I shall never strike a wrong note." He *may* say, though, "I have given whole recitals without a single technical slip." Anton Rubinstein, because of his great productiveness as a composer, often neglected his piano practice to such an extent that his colossal technic became impaired to a marked degree. This did not prevent him from gaining and keeping his rank as one of the two greatest piano virtuosos the world has known. It has been wittily said that "his wrong notes were better than the good notes of other pianists."

Why, then, should a pianist dread striking wrong notes, if he knows that his technical accuracy, through careful, competent training, has become mechanical and unconscious, and that even if he does strike a few wrong notes they will not imperil his success in the least! Indeed they will not. Beauty of touch and tone, dynamics, agogics, rhythm, accentuation, conception, interpretation, execution and rendition, these count!

Memory and technical accuracy being disposed of, there remains this fear: not to play as well as usual. This, if it happens, cannot be helped and should not disturb a performer.

No one can hope to go through life without swerving, in his performance, from the highest standard he can reach. His performance will always fluctuate in merit, reaching at times the apex of excellency and brilliancy, at others falling below it. The pianist's aim should be to increase the efficiency of his playing in such a manner that *the lowest limit of merit to which his playing can fall will be high enough for the public, good enough to compel success.*

Let a pianist who contemplates appearing in concert remember that his touch and tone, having been obtained through years of careful, loving attention given them, have become part of his mode of playing and that they *cannot* be suddenly changed. This holds good, too, for dynamics and agogics. It is inconceivable, nay impossible, that on the spur of the moment, the dynamic and agogic treatment of the piece to be played will become entirely different from what it was before. After a certain stage of development, it is reproduced *automatically*.

Thus, too, with every one of the other requisites of a beautiful performance; under the stress of nervousness, they may be slightly altered, but they can never be changed entirely. The result of matured study and of endless repetitions, they have become a *habit*.

The Pianist's Judgment of His Own Playing during a Public Performance

The judgment which a pianist brings to bear on his performance, *while he is playing*, is subject to curious changes and if faulty, may rob him of the necessary confidence and assurance.

To make this point clear, let us suppose that a pianist has heard somebody else play a piece which appeared to him very difficult and brilliant. He starts working on that piece; when he has succeeded in conquering all its difficulties and in playing it with ease, on that day, the impression of great difficulty and brilliancy which the piece made on him at the first hearing is lost forever. The fact that he can play it himself makes the piece seem easy to him. He is then apt, when playing for others, to try to revive his first reactions to this piece; in other words, he tries to "astonish himself" by playing certain passages faster or louder, by a more forceful accentuation than usual perhaps. Such a voluntary change in the manner of playing the piece is bound to bring undesirable and at times, disastrous, results.

A picture, once finished and approved, should not be touched up again. In like manner the pianist should confine himself to *reproduce,* to play again, in the way he has always played, every piece that forms part of his *repertoire.* Tempo, dynamics, accentuation, quality of expression--yes, his very gestures--let him simply reproduce them, and not suddenly, seek new, untried effects.

"But he had not that supreme gift of the artist, the knowledge of when to stop."

(Conan Doyle)

Any anxiety as to how "his piece" will be received by his audience works detrimentally on the playing of a performer. He should not ask himself: "Will the people applaud me, will they understand?" Rather should he think: "I am giving my all--the best my soul, heart, intelligence and physical energy can conjure. None can do more."

Audiences are apt to be as moody and capricious as single individuals who lack depth, a warm, genial disposition and a fair-minded, generous attitude towards others.

Every experienced concert artist knows that a piece that "takes well" on one occasion may leave the audience unmoved on another, even though the performance is of equal merit. These vagaries of audiences are found also in newspaper criticisms. Therefore it behooves an artist worthy of the name not to try to follow these inconstant moods, should they be made manifest (which does not always happen). He should, under all circumstances, adhere to the high ideals that gave birth to his conception of the piece. No matter what the musical, intellectual and emotional standard of his audience is, he should, at all times, remain *himself,* unconcerned as to the way his hearers will receive his performance.

It is only, as has been said before, when he believes that new, or different effects are advisable, that he may, in his study room, change his mode of playing.

Let us, finally, consider the meaning and effect of the words under the heading of this chapter.

We all know how temperament and fire, dash and abandon, vivify the playing of a pianist. They should, however, be governed by a keen intelligence, good judgment, and self-control.

A performer should thoroughly understand this. that he deserves no special credit for having temperament, because he has been born with it. He deserves praise only for having developed his temperament along the lines of aesthetic rules, and for knowing when to restrain it and when to let it have full sway.

There is a vast difference between temperament and temper! Yet it is the latter that some misguided persons indulge in, apparently in the belief that it denotes an artistic temperament!

Persons of a cold or phlegmatic nature find it easy to keep a steady control over their nerves and thereby over tempo, dynamics, accentuation and so on. Their playing, though, usually lacks the warmth, emotion and passion necessary to awaken response in the heart of the listener. The temperamental player satisfies these demands, but he often lacks the poise necessary to govern and regulate his fiery nature and through undue haste of tempos, shortening and hurrying of phrases and general restlessness, he often destroys all the good effect that his playing might achieve.

When to be fiery and dashing, and when to use restraint and care? On general principles, a performer may give free rein to his temperament when it is *safe,* technically, for him to do so, but he should not try to dash off passages that he has often missed in practice.

Considering the piece from the standpoint of the auditor, one should carefully note the passages where one is to *appear* deliberate in action, such as the striking of chords that require a special accentuation (first poising the hands, or holding them aloft, over the keys to be struck);

the beginnings of phrases or sections, especially after long rests, or holds, and before emphatic accents. Fiery chords and accents do not necessitate your taking chances of missing them in the passion and exaltation of your performance. A "lifted" chord, that is to say, a chord taken "out" of the keyboard usually sounds better than a chord struck "in" and the gesture of "lifting" or "coming out" of the keyboard may be as fiery and broad as desired; the accuracy of the chord is, meanwhile, assured.

Let a period of temperamental, passionate playing be followed by a period of *apparent*, as well as real, care and deliberation; and *vice versa*. You will then give to your auditors the impression of being master of yourself, of knowing how to control your feelings, yet of yielding at the proper moment to the impulse of your artistic self. Let the fundamental characteristics of your playing evidence prudence, "preparation of keys," but whenever the spirit or the style of the music demands it, whenever skips are unavoidable, then be courageous, dashing, trusting for accuracy to "mechanical" action, to the acquired "feeling of distance," (see the chapter on "Accuracy" Book II).

Be able, at any moment, to throw on the page of music which you are playing the searchlight of your "illuminative" memory. Be able, whenever you wish, to see every note; but trust, often, to your subconscious self, who guides faithfully, most of your actions in life. Realize that on every occasion your playing will be what it has become through patient study and efforts, and that any falling off as to the merit of the performance may seem big to you, who are performing, but very small, or not noticeable, to your auditors.

Confident in your ability, display that which, in the last analysis, sanctions your right to appear before others-- authority. Encourage freedom of attitude and mental relaxation, as well as physical, by avoiding a rigid, or never varying position of the body, while playing. At times lean over the keyboard, then away from it. Lean over to the left, or to the right; at times simply turn your head to the left or to the right; emphasize accents through the motion of your head or body; *have something to say*. (See the chapters on "Musical Prosody and Declamation" and "Rendition").

Remember that you have toiled and endured and sacrificed that you might content your heart's desire and become a worthy, perhaps a great, artist; that you are now among the chosen few, called upon to disclose to willing, grateful ears the beauties of the compositions which great minds have created. Remember that these works await silently the master hand that will bring them again to life, and that you have gained the *right* to be counted among the sincere, able and talented interpreters.

Banish, forever, the idea of fear ~~and~~ failure. *Live* at the piano the beautiful dreams that, throughout his life, every artist cherishes in his heart.

> "This above all; to thine own self be true,
> And it must follow, as the night the day,
> Thou canst not then be false to any man."
> (Shakespeare :- Hamlet, Act. 1, Scene 3)

You are on the concert-stage, facing an expectant multitude. Look now! Where are fear and failure? They have vanished, like shadows. Self-respect, confidence and courage surround you, and success and the joy of your art are yours.

The Problem of Success in Public Performance
by
LEOPOLD SCHMIDT

(This exceedingly valuable essay, by one of the most celebrated of German music critics, was written expressly for this work).

When the author of this work honored me with the request for a contribution, he expressed the desire that I discuss the requirements of a concert pianist from the standpoint of the critic.

The question, "What must the critic demand of every public performer?" is not a question of a special nature, but embraces the problem of the necessary attributes and preliminary qualifications in general; for the standard of the critic is no other than that of the teacher, his postulate being the sum of all that which is indispensable from a pedagogical, technical, musically-esthetic standpoint.

However, a competent critic is primarily in the position to observe the causes and effects from which depend the success or the failure of a concert. Success in public is a problem which is not always easy to solve, an art in itself, wherein, besides the unaccountable mood of the public, several factors must co-operate. And concerning this phase, much may indeed be said.

According to my experience, there are primarily three things which determine the success of an artist: His outward appearance; his program; and what I would like to term his inward relation to the music to be performed.

His outward personality*) -- that is, the manner of his appearance and conduct, is a matter the importance of which is often underestimated. Just as the dress of the performer must be neat and festive, yet without undue elaboration (a dress suited to a serious intellectual accomplishment, not frivolous), so his conduct must be in keeping with the dignity of the occasion.

Our relation to the artist, who for one evening is to hold sway over our attention, our imagination, is, to a certain extent, a personal one, and it is by no means an indifferent matter whether his appearance affects us sympathetically or not. Nothing is more distressing than ridiculous mannerisms in walking, in bowing, in sitting at the piano, or even in playing. Still, the virtuoso has a slight tendency to make known, with more or less unconscious gestures, his inspiration, the difficulty of a passage, or the abundance of his emotion. Just as injurious to true artistic effect, is the affectation of pronounced self-consciousness, the conduct of one who constantly seeks to draw attention to his own worthy person.

True knowledge does not need all this. The more unassumingly, modestly, and unconcernedly a performer appears, the more will he win our confidence. We like to see a man who, inwardly prepared, goes to his task with composure; for whom external trappings are only a necessity to be endured and who forgets everything about him as soon as he begins to play.

If a proper appearance and conduct are both prerequisites (which may be overlooked only in rare instances such as a master of towering significance), the skillful arrangement of the program is also a potent means of success. The choice of pieces to be performed must be considered from a subjective as well as from an objective standpoint. The artistic individuality of the performer is the deciding factor. If a composition does not "lie well" for a particular individuality, it does not belong on the program, no matter how effective it may be. Almost all

*) See chapter "Rendition" (A. J.)

talents are limited and each artist does well to know his limitations and should not allow himself to be led astray into fields where at best, he can only imitate. The lack of such self-criticism is often enough the cause of half, or even the entire failure.

The effect upon the public, is another viewpoint which must be considered. One must choose whether those compositions which one desires to play are actually suited to concert performance, whether they appeal to the taste, not of the mass, but of competent, serious minded contemporaries; whether they offer sufficient variety, climax, effective contrasts. The art of arranging a program wherein the lights and shadows are evenly distributed, which is not too bright and yet not monotonous, which with all its contrasts, still preserves its unity, is extremely difficult. Nowadays, this demand for "unity" has been very much emphasized, and recourse has been had to so-called "historical programs" which, no doubt, have solved many a difficulty owing to their prescribed continuity.

However, the concert hall is no classroom, and historical, biographical notices, or dates, have no place on programs. Even though we no longer live in the time of Liszt, who did not consider a sonata suitable for concert performance, but who played fantasias on opera themes, nevertheless, we should never forget that the concert, in its very nature, aims toward musical entertainment, and is no teaching institution. It is not the need for knowledge which is to be satisfied, but the desire for aesthetic enjoyment, and that desire is best satisfied, if, when arranging a program, one is governed exclusively by aesthetic principles. A musician of taste, of fine sensibilities, need consult only his feelings, provided that he has a sufficient knowledge of his literature, and he will choose rightly, both as to selection and grouping, thereby insuring to a certain extent, his success beforehand.

The main thing, that which makes for the ultimate decision is, of course, the third point: the art of interpretation. I am not considering the technic, facility, touch or memory of a pianist, all of which are taken for granted as prerequisites for success in public performance. Technical virtuosity in itself has earned fame and admiration for many, still it is rarely the only characteristic, since technical ability of a high order, from experience, is always coupled with musical talent. Then, too, it will satisfy only in such compositions where technic is primary, and that is a very limited field. In real music-- that is, music as an art of expression--each effect depends upon the inner musicianship of the performer. I demand of a pianist, appearing in public, above all that he differentiate between the styles of various periods and composers (as for example, the classic, romantic, and modern style, the style of Bach, Beethoven, Chopin and so on). Moreover, he must be able to prove his understanding of the formal structure and content of a composition in its utmost significance. In addition, I expect him to be at one with the composer--to have a sort of intangible inner-relationship with his work, which the audience will *feel* even though they may not be able to put an exact, critical finger upon it.

Every true work of art contains within it certain requirements for its presentation. We agree that there is a certain Standard, which is unquestioned by the Knowing, the breaking of which would mean arbitrariness. We also agree that within this Standard, there may be a wealth of variations, of interpretative possibilities, such as cannot be found by a strict adherence to the text or to the exact agogic and dynamic indications. And it is just this "Interpretation" which really makes the playing of an artist interesting. Where must the boundaries be drawn? Where lies the middle path between objective and subjective rendition?

A too great objectivity seems prosaic and leaves us cold; we not only desire to enjoy the composition, but also the personality of the interpreter. Exaggerated subjectivity meets the remonstrance of presumption and arouses differences of opinions.

It seems to me that the success of a concertising artist depends not so much upon what he gives as upon how he gives it. It depends upon whether his interpretation is the result of thought or of intuition. A too pronounced effort leaves us cold and estranged; the unconscious personal quality, be it ever so free, has the power of conviction and tears the listener along. The balance between subjective and objective representation is a matter of genius.

One sees that the problem of successful public performance is a very complex one and can never be definitely solved. No rules may be laid down, as all depends upon the individual and the power of his personality. These lines, for that reason, are merely meant to give the student an impetus; to lead him to lines of thought which may prove valuable to him in preparing for a career and in his subsequent activity.

Index of Preparatory Exercises and Examples Contained in the Seven Books of the Master School of Modern Piano Playing and Virtuosity

BEETHOVEN, LUDWIG VAN—*Continued*

BRAHMS, JOHANNES

BRAHMS, JOHANNES—*Continued*

BUSONI, FERRUCCIO

CHOPIN, FREDERICK

LIAPOUNOW, SERGE

LISZT, FRANZ

TABLE OF CONTENTS

BOOK I

BOOK II

BOOK II (Continued)

TABLE OF CONTENTS

BOOK III

BOOK IV

TABLE OF CONTENTS

BOOK IV (Continued)

BOOK IV (Continued)

TABLE OF CONTENTS

BOOK V

BOOK V (Continued)

TABLE OF CONTENTS

BOOK VI

BOOK VI (Continued)